GLOBE QUARTOS

THE ANTIPODES
RICHARD BROME

First printed: London, 1640

*This edition prepared by David Scott Kastan
and Richard Proudfoot*

GLOBE EDUCATION

NICK HERN BOOKS

www.

GLOBE QUARTOS

This edition of *The Antipodes*
first published in Great Britain
as a paperback original in 2000
by Nick Hern Books Limited
14 Larden Road, London W3 7ST

in association with

Globe Education
Shakespeare's Globe, New Globe Walk
London SE1 9DT

Typeset by Country Setting, Kingsdown, Kent CT14 8ES
Printed by CLE Print Ltd, Media House, Burrel Road,
St. Ives, Huntingdon,
Cambridgeshire PE27 3LE

A CIP catalogue record for this book is available from
the British Library

ISBN 978 1 85459 603 1

FSC
www.fsc.org
MIX
From responsible
sources
FSC® C019549

PREFACE

Over 400 plays written between 1567 and 1642 have survived in print. Few are now read and even fewer are performed. In 1995 Globe Education initiated a 30-year project to stage readings with professional casts of all the surviving texts so that audiences may once again hear plays by Barnes, Haughton, Shirley, Wilkins *et al.*

In 1997 Mark Rylance, Artistic Director of Shakespeare's Globe, included full productions of Beaumont and Fletcher's *The Maid's Tragedy* and Middleton's *A Chaste Maid in Cheapside* as part of the Globe Theatre's opening season. Over 30,000 people came to hear and see the two plays.

The popularity of the readings and the productions prompted Globe Education to approach Nick Hern to publish the texts being revived at the Globe to enable more people to read, study and, ideally, to produce them. Developments in computer typesetting combined with Simon Trussler's technical and bibliographical expertise have enabled editions to be published economically and quickly as *Globe Quartos*.

The first *Globe Quartos* were edited in 1998 by Nick de Somogyi. In 1999 an Editorial Board, composed of David Scott Kastan, Gordon McMullan and Richard Proudfoot, was established to oversee the series.

Globe Education is indebted to all those who have helped to give new life to old plays: production teams, actors, audiences, directors, editors, publishers and readers.

Patrick Spottiswoode
Director, Globe Education

EDITORIAL BOARD'S PREFACE

The aim of the series is to make once more available English plays of the late sixteenth and early seventeenth centuries that have long been out of print in affordable form or have been available to readers only in scholarly editions in academic libraries. The *Globe Quartos* texts are based on the most reliable surviving forms of these plays (usually the first printed editions). These have been fully edited and modernised so as to make them easily usable by actors and readers today. Editorial correction and emendation are undertaken where required by the state of the original. Extra stage directions added by editors and needed to make the action clear are enclosed in square brackets. Apostrophes in verse speeches indicate elision of syllables and reflect the metrical pattern of the line. Prefatory matter includes notes from the director or co-ordinator of the production or reading of the play at the Globe and a brief factual introduction by the editor. Glossarial notes (keyed to the text by line numbers) explain difficult or obsolete usages and offer brief comment on other points of interest or obscurity. Departures from the wording of the original are recorded in textual notes that identify the source of corrections or editorial emendations. The opening page of the text in the original on which the edition is based is reproduced in reduced facsimile. Extra material relevant to the understanding of the play may occasionally be included in an Appendix.

Acknowledgements

The editors wish to thank all those whose help has made it possible to produce this edition of Brome's *The Antipodes*, especially earlier editors of the play for their contribution to establishing and explaining the text and the British Library for permission to reprint the first text page of one of their copies of the 1640 quarto. They also wish to express their gratitude to Nicola Bennett for her help with the edition.

A Note from the Master of Play

Richard Brome was a manservant of Ben Jonson, probably his amanuensis and perhaps his literary protégé. He is inevitably compared with Jonson and has invariably suffered in the comparison: he is not as savage in his satiric thrust or as economic in his plotting and he lacks his master's intellectual wit. But Brome deserves to emerge from Jonson's shadow. He writes with great skill and craft and shows a mind more gentle and sympathetic, a heart more warm and forgiving of human nature than Jonson's. While recognising their foibles, Brome's generous spirit allows his characters to retain some of their dignity and sweetness.

The Antipodes is filled with many satiric scenes that illuminate the everyday life of people living in the Caroline period. It is a world of topsy-turvy, a world subverted, turned upside down. What's happening? Who's who? When is it 'then' and when is it 'now'? Grand lords dress humbly, servants sumptuously. Actors portray servants, who portray actors, who assume roles and genders other than their own. Doctors use psychology instead of medicine to cure problems. Among other inventions, The Antipodes presents a portrait of one of the first practising psychiatrists on the English stage.

There is no getting away from the fact that nowadays there are parts of The Antipodes which may work on the printed page, but do not on the stage. In the Globe production, we cut some of those scenes from Brome's original published script which, to make their satiric point, depend upon the immediate recognition of seventeenth-century archetypes, occasions when Brome sets up the metaphor but fails to dramatise it. For instance, the principal characters view the scene presented in the play-within-the-play as an audience would, but they are seldom drawn in or interact with the satiric characters being presented. When one strips away the satiric observations that have not been theatricalised, there emerges a leaner play that nevertheless succeeds in revealing a fun-filled and fresh observation of period behaviour and social satire. One gains some confidence and comfort in cutting and pruning from a printed apology (or disclaimer) of the author in the first printed version of the play. The players apparently discovered something in the playing that had escaped the author. At the same time, one is struck by how much of human nature, particularly as it is revealed in the relationships and transactions between people, remains the same.

Brome created a world of antic humour and anarchic suspension of expec-
tations that make for a screwball comedy. The viewer is left wondering: who
are the doctors and who the patients? Who is slightly 'off', who deeply
troubled? His imagination, energy and theatrical suspense are unflagging.
I particularly enjoy his last revelations in the testing of Diana, Joyless's young
wife. Her marital fidelity is put to the test of a mock seduction by Lord Letoy,
who turns out to be her father! It is a scene that recalls a similar episode in
Jonson's *Volpone*. This is followed by a preposterous but delightful reconci-
liation scene in the same vein as those which close *The Winter's Tale* and *Pericles*,
but without their sense of magic and wonder. Dr Hughball seems to cure
Peregrine's madness by taking him deeper into a world of topsy-turvy and thus
restoring by degrees his sense of what is the norm:

> Observe the doctor's art.
> First, he has shifted your son's known disease
> Of madness into folly and has wrought him
> As far short of a competent reason as
> He was of late beyond it . . .
> So is a madman made a fool before
> Art can take hold of him to wind him up
> Into his proper centre, or the medium
> From which he flew beyond himself.

However, carnal knowledge is finally the means to bring the patient to his
senses. Peregrine is manoeuvred into thinking he is a king married to a queen
who is his real wife, Martha. The marriage is finally consummated (after three
celibate years) and Peregrine is restored to reason. So, without making a particularly moral or satiric point, sex becomes the engine for recovery – not a bad
idea, and one that fuels my impression of the play as an antic, anarchic place
where logic does not rule. Lord Letoy and Dr Hughball use the art of the
theatre, an unreal and artificial world, to bring Peregrine to an acknow-
ledgement of and presence in the real world.

The theatre, by transporting our minds and psyches to worlds real or
imagined, has always been effective as a healing art; it can transcend limits and
boundaries and reach deep into the heart and soul. Brome recognised this, and
in *The Antipodes* created a play – and a play-within-a-play – which conjures up
a frolicsome world of nonsense and common sense.

Gerald Freedman
Master of Play

THE ANTIPODES

Cast of the play, adapted by Gerald Freedman,
which opened at Shakespeare's Globe on 12 August 2000

Blaze, a herald painter	Tim Preece
Doctor Hughball, a doctor of Physic	Geoffrey Beevers
Barbara, wife of Blaze	Joanna McCallum
Joyless, an old country gentleman	James Hayes
Peregrine, son of Joyless	Harry Gostelow
Diana, wife of Joyless	Penny Layden
Martha, wife of Peregrine	Karen Tomlin
Letoy, a fantastic lord	Tim Woodward
Quailpipe	Roger Gartland
Byplay, a conceited servant of Letoy	Mark Lockyer
Truelock, a close friend of Letoy	Chris Tranchell
Followers of Letoy	Tim Block
	Dragan Micanovic
	Jan Knightley
	Mark Rylance
	David Phelan
	Leader Hawkins

Other roles played by members of the company

Musicians	Martin Allen
	Phil Hopkins
	Dai Pritchard
	Keith Thompson
	Claire van Kampen

Master of Play	Gerald Freedman
Assistant to Master of Play	Jeremy Skidmore
Master of Verse	Giles Block

Master of Clothing and Properties	Jenny Tiramani
Assistant to Master of Clothing	Seral Ibrahim
Master of Music	Claire van Kampen
Master of Dance	Sian Williams
Company Manager	Marian Spon
Stage Managers	Sid Charlton
	Tamzin Gibb
	Bryan Paterson
	Helen Wallis

Editor's Introduction

Although not very well known today, Richard Brome was a successful playwright of the 1630s and early 1640s, before the theatres were closed by parliamentary order in September 1642. As early as 1614, Brome was in London employed by Ben Jonson as a servant. He thrived in Jonson's household, becoming the writer's protégé and friend. He wrote for various dramatic companies in the early 1630s, including the King's Men who played at the Globe and the Blackfriars. In 1635, Brome signed a contract to serve as the company playwright for a troupe of actors that played the Salisbury Court theatre. Editions of at least fifteen of his plays reached print before 1660, including two collected volumes of five plays each, one published in 1653 (and popular enough to be reissued the following year) and one in 1659.

The Antipodes was written sometime in 1636, during a seventeen-month period when the theatres were closed on account of a serious outbreak of plague. The play shows Brome's deep indebtedness to his friend Jonson, who died in 1637. 'Jonson's alive!', wrote one admirer of Brome's achievement, in a commendatory poem in the 1640 quarto. The spirited play indeed seems very like a Jonson comedy, with the densely populated and complex plot of Jonson's best plays, and something too of Jonson's moral commitments. For each playwright, the drama serves as a form of therapy: characters, and the audience itself, are led to see their follies and are given opportunities to partake of a cure. The hypocrisies and affectations of Brome's own London are laid before the audience's view for recognition and amelioration. But where Jonson's comic therapy is often a harsh purgative, Brome's 'medicine of the mind' works by the operation of a gentle wit, no doubt more appropriate for a city recently suffering the plague's ravages.

Peregrine is the play's most obvious patient. He is obsessed with the marvels of travellers' reports, living in a world of 'Mere shadowy phantasms, or fantastic dreams'. The Doctor's cure, achieved with the help of Lord Letoy's acting company, is to convince Peregrine that he has travelled to the Antipodes, a place far stranger than even the strangest of travellers' tales. The land of the Antipodes, as it appears in Letoy's play-within-a-play, is a version of London itself, exhibiting its foibles and crimes, and Peregrine comes to see the need to right this topsy-turvy world. Both Peregrine and the audience are led to reject an empty escapism in favour of a willingness to see their own world with a generous clarity. The play ends with a triumph of harmony, with 'Wit against Folly, Love against Jealousy, / Wine against Melancholy, and 'gainst Madness, Health'. If the play successfully exposes some of the social and political failings of Caroline England, it also argues for the redeeming social and emotional value of the theatre itself.

Though Brome had signed a contract in 1635 to write exclusively for the Salisbury Court players, *The Antipodes* was in fact written in direct violation of the company's contractual claims on the playwright's services. It was written for a rival company led by William Beeston and 'intended for the Cock-pit Stage', as an epistle to the 'Curteous Reader' in the 1640 quarto makes clear; and it seems almost certainly to be the cause of a complaint brought by the Salisbury Court players against Brome for violating the clause in his contract enjoining him from giving 'any play or any part of a play to any other players or playhouse'.

Brome admitted his offence, defending his actions by noting that he had not been paid any of his stipulated salary during the plague outbreak that had closed the theatres from May of 1636 until early October in 1637. With no income from the Salisbury Court, Brome approached Beeston, who gave him £6 for a play that Brome would write for the players at the Cockpit. Learning of this, the Salisbury Court players threatened Brome with a legal action to protect their rights to his work. Reluctantly, Brome recovered his play from Beeston, and it was finally, as the title page of the 1640 edition states, successfully 'acted in the yeare 1638, by the Queenes Majesties Servants, at Salisbury Court in Fleet-Street'.

The Antipodes was entered in the Stationers' Register on 19 March 1640, and published that year, printed by John Okes for Francis Constable. Twenty-three copies of the 1640 quarto have survived, and this modernised edition used the second British Library copy (shelfmark 162 c.13) as its control text.

David Scott Kastan

THE ANTIPODES

DEDICATORY EPISTLE

To
The Right Honourable
William, Earl of Hertford, &c.

My lord,

The long experience I have had of your Honour's favourable
intentions towards me hath compelled me to this presumption.
But I hope your goodness will be pleased to pardon what your
benignity was the cause of, viz., the error of my dedication. Had
your candour not encouraged me in this, I had been innocent;
yet, I beseech you, think not I intend it any other than your   10
recreation at your retirement from your weighty employments,
and to be the declaration of your gracious encouragements towards
me, and the testimony of my gratitude. If the public view of
the world entertain it with no less welcome than that private
one of the stage already has given it, I shall be glad the world
owes you the thanks. If it meet with too severe construction,
I hope your protection. What hazards so ever it shall justle with,
my desires are it may pleasure your lordship in the perusal, which
 is the only ambition he is conscious of who is,

My lord,   20
Your Honour's humbly devoted
Richard Brome

4

COMMENDATORY VERSES

To censuring Critics on the approved Comedy,
The Antipodes

Jonson's alive! The world admiring stands,
And to declare his welcome there, shake hands,
Apollo's pensioners may wipe their eyes
And stifle their abortive elegies;
Taylor his goose quill may abjure again,
And to make paper dear, scribbling refrain;
For sure there's cause of neither. Jonson's ghost
Is not a tenant i'the Elysian coast,
But vex'd with too much scorn at your dispraise,
Silently stole unto a grove of bays.   10
Therefore bewail your errors, and entreat
He will return unto the former seat,
Whence he was often pleas'd to feed your ear
With the choice dainties of his theatre.
But I much fear he'll not be easily won
To leave his bower, where grief and he alone
Do spend their time, to see how vainly we
Accept old toys for a new comedy.
Therefore repair to him, and praise each line
Of his *Volpone, Sejanus, Catiline*.   20
But stay, and let me tell you where he is:
He sojourns in his Brome's *Antipodes*.

C.G.

To the Author on his Comedy,
The Antipodes

Steer'd by the hand of Fate o'er swelling seas,
Methought I landed on th'Antipodes,
Where I was straight a stranger; for 'tis thus:
Their feet do tread against the tread of us.
My scull mistook; thy book, being in my hand,
Hurried my soul to th'Antipodean strand,
Where I did feast my fancy and mine eyes
With such variety of rarities,
That I perceive thy muse frequents some shade
Might be a grove for a Pierian maid.   10
Let idiots prate; it boots not what they say.
Th'Antipodes to wit and learning may
Have ample priv'lege, for among that crew
I know there's not a man can judge of you.

Rob. Chamberlain

Dramatis Personae

The Persons in the Play

[PROLOGUE]

BLAZE	*an herald painter*
JOYLESS	*an old country gentleman*
[DOCTOR] *Hughball*	*a doctor of physic*
BARBARA	*wife to Blaze*
MARTHA	*wife to Peregrine*
LETOY	*a fantastic lord*
QUAILPIPE	*his curate*
PEREGRINE	*son to Joyless*
DIANA	*wife to Joyless*
BYPLAY	*a conceited servant to Letoy*
TRUELOCK	*a close friend to Letoy*

10

Followers of the Lord Letoy's, who are actors in the byplay

[The action is set in London, in the houses of Blaze and Lord Letoy.]

[*Enter*] *the* PROLOGUE

Opinion, which our author cannot court
For the dear daintiness of it, has of late
From the old way of plays possess'd a sort
Only to run to those that carry state
In scene magnificent and language high,
And clothes worth all the rest, except the action.
And such are only good, those leaders cry;
And into that belief draw on a faction
That must despise all sportive, merry wit,
Because some such great play had none in it.   10

But it is known (peace to their memories)
The poets late sublimed from our age,
Who best could understand and best devise
Works that must ever live upon the stage,
Did well approve and lead this humble way
Which we are bound to travel in tonight.
And though it be not trac'd so well as they
Discover'd it by true Phoebean light,
Pardon our just ambition yet that strive
To keep the weakest branch o'th' stage alive.   20

I mean the weakest in their great esteem
That count all slight that's under us, or nigh,
And only those for worthy subjects deem,
Fetch'd, or reach'd at, at least, from far or high,
When low and homebred subjects have their use
As well as those fetch'd from on high or far.
And 'tis as hard a labour for the muse
To move the earth as to dislodge a star.
See yet those glorious plays, and let their sight   29
Your admiration move; these, your delight.   [*Exit*]

ACT 1, SCENE 1

[Enter] BLAZE *[and]* JOYLESS

Blaze	To me, and to the city, sir, you are welcome,
	And so are all about you. We have long
	Suffer'd the want of such fair company.
	But now that time's calamity has given way,
	Thanks to high providence, to your kinder visits,
	We are – like half-pin'd wretches that have lain
	Long on the planks of sorrow, strictly tied
	To a forc'd abstinence from the sight of friends –
	The sweetlier fill'd with joy.
Joyless	Alas, I bring
	Sorrow too much with me to fill one house 10
	In the sad number of my family.
Blaze	Be comforted, good sir. My house, which now
	You may be pleas'd to call your own, is large
	Enough to hold you all. And, for your sorrows,
	You came to lose 'em, and I hope the means
	Is readily at hand. The doctor's coming,
	Who, as by letters I advertis'd you,
	Is the most promising man to cure your son
	The kingdom yields. It will astonish you
	To hear the marvels he hath done in cures 20
	Of such distracted ones as is your son,
	And not so much by bodily physic – no,
	He sends few recipes to th'apothecaries! –
	As medicine of the mind, which he infuses
	So skilfully, yet by familiar ways,
	That it begets both wonder and delight

In his observers, while the stupid patient
Finds health at unawares.

Joyless   You speak well of him.
Yet I may fear my son's long-grown disease
Is such he hath not met with.

Blaze   Then I'll tell you, sir.   30
He cur'd a country gentleman that fell mad
For spending of his land before he sold it;
That is, 'twas sold to pay his debts – all went
That way for a dead horse, as one would say!
He had not money left to buy his dinner
Upon that wholesale day. This was a cause
Might make a gentleman mad, you'll say; and him
It did, as mad as landless squire could be.
This doctor by his art remov'd his madness
And mingled so much wit among his brains   40
That, by the overflowing of it merely,
He gets and spends five hundred pound a year now
As merrily as any gentleman
In Derbyshire. I name no man; but this
Was pretty well, you'll say.

Joyless   My son's disease
Grows not that way.

Blaze   There was a lady mad –
I name no lady – but stark mad she was
As any in the country, city, or almost
In court could be.

Joyless   How fell she mad?

Blaze   With study,
Tedious and painful study. And for what   50
Now, can you think?

Joyless   For painting, or new fashions?
I cannot think for the philosopher's stone.

Blaze	No, 'twas to find a way to love her husband,
	Because she did not, and her friends rebuk'd her.
Joyless	Was that so hard to find, if she desired it?
Blaze	She was seven years in search of it and could not,
	Though she consum'd his whole estate by it.
Joyless	'Twas he was mad then.
Blaze	No, he was not born

With wit enough to lose! But mad was she
Until this doctor took her into cure.   60
And now she lies as lovingly on a flockbed
With her own knight as she had done on down
With many others – but I name no parties.
Yet this was well, you'll say.

Joyless   Would all were well!

Blaze Then, sir, of officers and men of place,
Whose senses were so numb'd they understood not
Bribes from due fees and fell on praemunires,
He has cur'd divers that can now distinguish
And know both when and how to take of both,
And grow most safely rich by't. T'other day   70
He set the brains of an attorney right
That were quite topsy-turvy overturn'd
In a pitch o'er the bar, so that, poor man,
For many moons he knew not whether he
Went on his heels or's head, till he was brought
To this rare doctor. Now he walketh again
As upright in his calling as the boldest
Amongst 'em. This was well, you'll say.

Joyless   'Tis much.

Blaze And then for horn-mad citizens, my neighbours,
He cures them by the dozens, and we live   80
As gently with our wives as rams with ewes.

Joyless	'We' do, you say – were you one of his patients?
Blaze	[*aside*] 'Slid, he has almost catch'd me. – No, sir, no.
	I name no parties, I, but wish you merry.
	I strain to make you so, and could tell forty
	Notable cures of his to pass the time
	Until he comes.
Joyless	But, pray, has he the art
	To cure a husband's jealousy?
Blaze	Mine, sir, he did – [*aside*] 'Sfoot, I am catch'd again.
Joyless	But still you name no party. Pray, how long, 90
	Good Master Blaze, has this so famous doctor,
	Whom you so well set out, been a professor?
Blaze	Never, in public; nor endures the name
	Of doctor – though I call him so – but lives
	With an odd lord in town, that looks like no lord.
	My doctor goes more like a lord than he.

                 Enter DOCTOR [*Hughball*]

	Oh, welcome, sir. I sent mine own wife for you;
	Ha' you brought her home again?
Doctor	She's in your house
	With gentlewomen who seem to lodge here.
Blaze	Yes, sir, this gentleman's wife and his son's wife. 100
	They all ail something; but his son, 'tis thought,
	Is falling into madness, and is brought
	Up by his careful father to the town here
	To be your patient. Speak with him about it.
Doctor	[*to* JOYLESS] How do you find him, sir? Does his disease
	Take him by fits, or is it constantly
	And at all times the same?
Joyless	For the most part
	It is only inclining still to worse

As he grows more in days. By all the best
Conjectures we have met with in the country   110
'Tis found a most deep melancholy.

Doctor   Of what years is he?

Joyless   Of five and twenty, sir.

Doctor   Was it born with him? Is it natural
Or accidental? Have you or his mother
Been so at any time affected?

Joyless   Never.
Not she unto her grave; nor I till then
Knew what a sadness meant, though since I have,
In my son's sad condition, and some crosses
In my late marriage, which at further time
I may acquaint you with.

Blaze   [aside]   The old man's jealous   120
Of his young wife! I find him by the question
He put to me erewhile.

Doctor   Is your son married?

Joyless   Divers years since; for we had hope a wife
Might have restrain'd his travailing thoughts and so
Have been a means to cure him, but it fail'd us.

Doctor   What has he in his younger years been most
Addicted to? What study or what practice?

Joyless   You have now, sir, found the question which, I think,
Will lead you to the ground of his distemper.   129

Doctor   That's the next way to the cure. Come, quickly, quickly.

Joyless   In tender years he always lov'd to read
Reports of travels and of voyages.
And when young boys like him would tire themselves
With sports and pastimes and restore their spirits

Again by meat and sleep, he would whole days
And nights (sometimes by stealth) be on such books
As might convey his fancy round the world.

Doctor   Very good; on.

Joyless   When he grew up towards twenty,
His mind was all on fire to be abroad;
Nothing but travel still was all his aim.   140
There was no voyage or foreign expedition
Be said to be in hand, but he made suit
To be made one in it. His mother and
Myself oppos'd him still in all and, strongly
Against his will, still held him in and won
Him into marriage, hoping that would call
In his extravagant thoughts. But all prevail'd not,
Nor stay'd him – though at home – from travelling
So far beyond himself that now, too late,
I wish he had gone abroad to meet his fate.   150

Doctor   Well, sir, upon good terms I'll undertake
Your son. Let's see him.

Joyless   Yet there's more: his wife, sir.

Doctor   I'll undertake her too. Is she mad too?

Blaze   They'll ha' mad children, then!

Doctor   Hold you your peace.

Joyless   Alas, the danger is they will have none.
He takes no joy in her and she no comfort
In him; for though they have been three years wed,
They are yet ignorant of the marriage bed.

Doctor   I shall find her the madder of the two, then.

Joyless   Indeed, she's full of passion, which she utters   160
By the effects, as diversely as several
Objects reflect upon her wand'ring fancy:

Sometimes in extreme weepings, and anon
In vehement laughter; now in sullen silence,
And presently in loudest exclamations.

Doctor   Come, let me see 'em, sir. I'll undertake
Her too. Ha' you any more? How does your wife?

Joyless   Some other time for her.

Doctor   I'll undertake
Her too. And you yourself, sir, by your favour
And some few yellow spots which I perceive   170
About your temples, may require some counsel.

               Enter BARBARA

Blaze   [*aside*] So, he has found him.

Joyless   But my son, my son, sir!

Blaze   Now, Bab, what news?

Barbara   There's news too much within
For any homebred Christian understanding.

Joyless   How does my son?

Barbara   He is in travail, sir.

Joyless   His fit's upon him?

Barbara   Yes. Pray, Doctor Hughball,
Play the man-midwife and deliver him
Of his huge tympany of news – of monsters,
Pygmies and giants, apes and elephants,
Gryphons and crocodiles, men upon women   180
And women upon men, the strangest doings –
As far beyond all Christendom as 'tis to't.

Doctor   How, how?

Barbara   Beyond the moon and stars, I think,
Or Mount in Cornwall either.

Blaze	[*aside*] How prettily like a fool she talks! An she were not mine own wife, I could be So taken with her.
Doctor	'Tis most wondrous strange.
Barbara	He talks much of the kingdom of Cathaya, Of one Great Khan and goodman Prester John (Whate'er they be), and says that Khan's a clown 190 Unto the John he speaks of; and that John Dwells up almost at Paradise. But sure his mind Is in a wilderness, for there he says Are geese that have two heads apiece, and hens That bear more wool upon their backs than sheep –
Doctor	O, Mandeville. Let's to him. Lead the way, sir.
Barbara	And men with heads like hounds!
Doctor	Enough, enough.
Barbara	You'll find enough within, I warrant ye.

            Exeunt DOCTOR, BLAZE *and* JOYLESS

        Enter MARTHA

[*Aside*] And here comes the poor mad gentleman's wife,
Almost as mad as he. She haunts me all   200
About the house to impart something to me.
Poor heart, I guess her grief and pity her.
To keep a maidenhead three years after marriage
Under wed-lock and key! Insufferable! Monstrous!
It turns into a wolf within the flesh,
Not to be fed with chickens and tame pigeons.
I could wish maids be warn'd by't not to marry
Before they have wit to lose their maidenheads,
For fear they match with men whose wits are past it.
What a sad look! And what a sigh was there! –   210
Sweet Mistress Joyless, how is't with you now?

Martha	When I shall know, I'll tell. Pray tell me first, How long have you been married?
Barbara	[*aside*] Now she is on it. – Three years, forsooth.
Martha	And, truly, so have I; We shall agree, I see.
Barbara	If you'll be merry.
Martha	No woman merrier, now I have met with one Of my condition. Three years married, say you? Ha, ha, ha!
Barbara	[*aside*] What ails she, trow?
Martha	Three years married! Ha, ha, ha!
Barbara	Is that a laughing matter?
Martha	'Tis just my story. 219 And you have had no child; that's still my story. Ha, ha, ha!
Barbara	Nay, I have had two children.
Martha	Are you sure on't? Or does your husband only tell you so? Take heed o'that, for husbands are deceitful.
Barbara	But I am o'the surer side. I am sure I groan'd for mine and bore 'em, when at best He but believes he got 'em.
Martha	Yet both he And you may be deceiv'd, for now I'll tell you, My husband told me, fac'd me down and stood on't, We had three sons, and all great travellers – That one had shook the Great Turk by the beard. 230 I never saw 'em, nor am I such a fool To think that children can be got and born, Train'd up to men, and then sent out to travel, And the poor mother never know nor feel Any such matter. There's a dream indeed!

Barbara   Now you speak reason, and 'tis nothing but
            Your husband's madness that would put that dream
            Into you.

Martha   He may put dreams into me, but
            He ne'er put child, nor anything towards it yet
            To me to making. (*Weeps*) Something, sure, belongs   240
            To such a work; for I am past a child
            Myself to think they are found in parsley beds,
            Strawberry banks or rosemary bushes, though
            I must confess I have sought and search'd such places,
            Because I would fain have had one.

Barbara   [*aside*]   'Las, poor fool!

Martha   Pray tell me, for I think nobody hears us,
            How came you by your babes? I cannot think
            Your husband got them you.

Barbara   [*aside*]   Fool, did I say?
            She is a witch, I think. – Why not my husband?
            Pray, can you charge me with another man?   250

Martha   Nor with him neither. Be not angry, pray now;
            For were I now to die, I cannot guess
            What a man does in child-getting. I remember
            A wanton maid once lay with me, and kiss'd
            And clipp'd and clapp'd me strangely, and then wish'd
            That I had been a man to have got her with child.
            What must I then ha' done, or, good now, tell me,
            What has your husband done to you?

Barbara   [*aside*]   Was ever
            Such a poor piece of innocence – three years married! –
            Does not your husband use to lie with you?   260

Martha   Yes, he does use to lie with me, but he does not
            Lie with me to use me as he should, I fear;
            Nor do I know to teach him. Will you tell me?

I'll lie with you and practise, if you please.
Pray take me for a night or two, or take
My husband and instruct him – but one night.
Our country folks will say you London wives
Do not lie every night with your own husbands.

Barbara   Your country folks should have done well to ha' sent
           Some news by you! But I trust none told you there   270
           We use to leave our fools to lie with madmen.

Martha   Nay, now again you're angry.

Barbara   No, not I,
           But rather pity your simplicity.
           Come, I'll take charge and care of you –

Martha   I thank you.

Barbara   And wage my skill against my doctor's art
           Sooner to ease you of these dangerous fits
           Than he shall rectify your husband's wits.

Martha   Indeed, indeed, I thank you.   *Exeunt*

ACT 1, SCENE 2

[Enter] LETOY, *[shabbily dressed, and]* BLAZE

Letoy   Why, brought'st thou not mine arms and pedigree
           Home with thee, Blaze, mine honest herald's painter?

Blaze   I have not yet, my lord, but all's in readiness,
           According to the herald's full directions.

Letoy   But has he gone to the root; has he deriv'd me
           Ex origine, ab antiquo? Has he fetch'd me
           Far enough, Blaze?

Blaze	Full four descents beyond
	The conquest, my good lord, and finds that one
	Of your French ancestry came in with the Conqueror.

Letoy   Jeffrey Letoy; 'twas he from whom the English   10
Letoys have our descent, and here have took
Such footing that we'll never out while France
Is France, and England England,
And the sea passable to transport a fashion.
My ancestors and I have been beginners
Of all new fashions in the court of England
From before *primo Ricardi Secundi*
Until this day.

Blaze   [*pointing at Letoy's clothes*] I cannot think, my lord,
They'll follow you in this though.

Letoy   Mark the end.
I am without a precedent for my humour.   20
But is it spread and talk'd of in the town?

Blaze   It is, my lord, and laugh'd at by a many.

Letoy   I am more beholding to them than all the rest.
Their laughter makes me merry; others' mirth
And not mine own it is that feeds me, that
Battens me as poor men's cost does usurers.
But tell me, Blaze, what say they of me, ha?

Blaze   They say, my lord, you look more like a pedlar
Than like a lord, and live more like an emperor.

Letoy   Why, there they ha' me right! Let others shine   30
Abroad in cloth o'baudkin; my broadcloth
Pleases mine eye as well, my body better.
Besides, I'm sure 'tis paid for, to their envy.
I buy with ready money and at home here
With as good meat, as much magnificence,

As costly pleasures and as rare delights,
Can satisfy my appetite and senses
As they with all their public shows and braveries.
They run at ring and tilt 'gainst one another;
I and my men can play a match at football,   40
Wrestle a handsome fall and pitch the bar,
And crack the cudgels, and a pate sometimes.
'Twould do you good to see't.

Blaze   More than to feel't!

Letoy   They hunt the deer, the hare, the fox, the otter,
Polecats, or harlots, what they please, whilst I
And my mad grigs, my men, can run at base
And breathe ourselves at barley-break and dancing.

Blaze   Yes, my lord, i'th' country, when you are there.

Letoy   And now I am here i'th' city, sir, I hope
I please myself with more choice home delights   50
Than most men of my rank.

Blaze   I know, my lord,
Your house in substance is an amphitheatre
Of exercise and pleasure.

Letoy   Sir, I have
For exercises, fencing, dancing, vaulting,
And for delight, music of all best kinds.
Stage plays and masques are nightly my pastimes,
And all within myself: my own men are
My music and my actors. I keep not
A man or boy but is of quality;
The worst can sing, or play his part o'th' viols,   60
And act his part, too, in a comedy,
For which I lay my bravery on their backs.
And where another lord undoes his followers,
I maintain mine like lords. And there's my bravery.

Hautboys. A service, as for dinner, pass over the stage, borne by many servitors
richly apparelled, doing honour to LETOY *as they pass. Exeunt*

	Now tell me, Blaze, look these like pedlar's men?

Blaze   Rather an emperor's, my lord.

Letoy   I tell thee,
These lads can act the emperors' lives all over,
And Shakespeare's chronicled histories to boot;
And were that Caesar, or that English earl,
That lov'd a play and player so well, now living,   70
I would not be outvied in my delights.

Blaze   My lord, 'tis well.

Letoy   I love the quality of playing, I.
I love a play with all my heart, a good one;
And a player that's a good one too, with all my heart.
As for the poets, no men love them, I think,
And therefore I write all my plays myself,
And make no doubt some of the court will follow
Me in that too. Let my fine lords
Talk o'their horse-tricks and their jockeys   80
That can out-talk them. Let the gallants boast
Their May-games, play-games and their mistresses;
I love a play in my plain clothes, I,
And laugh upon the actors in their brave ones.

Enter QUAILPIPE

Quailpipe   My lord, your dinner stays prepar'd.

Letoy   Well, well,
Be you as ready with your grace as I
Am for my meat, and all is well.   *Exit* QUAILPIPE
                              Blaze, we have rambled
From the main point this while: it seems by his letter
My doctor's busy at thy house.
I know who's there beside. Give him this ring;   90

	Tell him it wants a finger. Farewell, good Blaze. [*Exit*]
Blaze	'Tell him it wants a finger?' My small wit
	Already finds what finger it must fit. [*Exit*]

ACT 1, SCENE 3

Enter DOCTOR, PEREGRINE, *a book in his hand,* JOYLESS
[*and*] DIANA. *A bowl* [*of wine*] *on the table*

Doctor
Sir, I applaud your noble disposition
And even adore the spirit of travel in you,
And purpose to wait on it through the world,
In which I shall but tread again the steps
I heretofore have gone.

Peregrine
                      All the world o'er
Ha' you been already?

Doctor
                      Over and under too.

Peregrine
In the Antipodes?

Doctor
                   Yes, through and through;
No isle nor angle in that nether world
But I have made discovery of. Pray, sir, sit.   9
[*To* JOYLESS] And, sir, be you attentive. I will warrant
His speedy cure, without the help of Galen,
Hippocrates, Avicen or Dioscorides.

Diana
A rare man! Husband, truly, I like his person
As well as his rare skill.

Joyless
                 In to your chamber!
I do not like your liking of men's persons.

Doctor
Nay, lady, you may stay. Hear and admire,
If you so please, but make no interruptions.

Joyless	[*aside to* DIANA] And let no looser words, or wand'ring look,
	Bewray an intimation of the slight
	Regard you bear your husband, lest I send you 20
	Upon a further pilgrimage than he
	Feigns to convey my son.
Diana	Oh, jealousy!
Doctor	Do you think, sir, to th'Antipodes such a journey?
Peregrine	I think there's none beyond it; and that Mandeville,
	Whose excellent work this is, [*shows him his book*]
	was th'only man
	That e'er came near it.
Doctor	Mandeville went far.
Peregrine	Beyond all English legs that I can read of.
Doctor	What think you, sir, of Drake, our famous countryman?
Peregrine	Drake was a didapper to Mandeville.
	Ca'ndish, and Hawkins, Frobisher, all our voyagers 30
	Went short of Mandeville. But had he reach'd
	To this place here [*finds a place in the book*]
	– yes, here, this wilderness –
	And seen the trees of the sun and moon, that speak,
	And told King Alexander of his death, he then
	Had left a passage ope for travellers
	That now is kept and guarded by wild beasts:
	Dragons, and serpents, elephants white and blue,
	Unicorns, and lions of many colours,
	And monsters more as numberless as nameless.
Doctor	Stay there –
Peregrine	Read here else. Can you read? 40
	Is it not true?
Doctor	No truer than I ha' seen't.

Diana	Ha' you been there, sir? Ha' you seen those trees?
Doctor	And talk'd with 'em and tasted of their fruit.
Peregrine	Read here again then: it is written here That you may live four or five hundred year.
Diana	Brought you none of that fruit home with you, sir?
Joyless	You would have some of't, would you, to have hope T'outlive your husband by't?
Diana	I'd ha't for you, In hope you might outlive your jealousy.
Doctor	Your patience both, I pray. I know the grief 50 You both do labour with and how to cure it.
Joyless	Would I had given you half my land 'twere done.
Diana	Would I had given him half my love to settle The t'other half free from encumbrances Upon my husband.
Doctor	Do not think it strange, sir. I'll make your eyes witnesses of more Than I relate, if you'll but travel with me. You hear me not deny that all is true That Mandeville delivers of his travels; Yet I myself may be as well believ'd. 60
Peregrine	Since you speak reverently of him, say on.
Doctor	Of Europe I'll not speak; 'tis too near home. Who's not familiar with the Spanish garb, Th'Italian shrug, French cringe and German hug? Nor will I trouble you with my observations Fetch'd from Arabia, Paphlagonia, Mesopotamia, Mauritania, Syria, Thessalia, Persia, India, All still is too near home. Though I have touch'd

The clouds upon the Pyrenean mountains,   70
And been on Paphos Isle, where I have kiss'd
The image of bright Venus, all is still
Too near home to be boasted.

Diana   [*aside*]   That I like
Well in him too; he will not boast of kissing
A woman too near home.

Doctor   These things in me
Are poor. They sound in a far traveller's ear
Like the reports of those that beggingly
Have put out on returns from Edinburgh,
Paris, or Venice, or perhaps Madrid,
Whither a milliner may with half a nose   80
Smell out his way, and is not near so difficult
As for some man in debt, and unprotected,
To walk from Charing Cross to th'old Exchange.
No: I will pitch no nearer than th'Antipodes,
That which is farthest distant, foot to foot
Against our region.

Diana   What, with their heels upwards?
Bless us! How scape they breaking o'their necks?

Doctor   They walk upon firm earth as we do here
And have the firmament over their heads,
As we have here.

Diana   And yet just under us!   90
Where is hell then? If they whose feet are towards us
At the lower part of the world have heaven too
Beyond their heads, where's hell?

Joyless   You may find that
Without enquiry. Cease your idle questions.

Diana   Sure hell's above ground, then, in jealous husbands!

Peregrine   What people, sir – I pray, proceed – what people

Are they of the Antipodes? Are they not such
As Mandeville writes of, without heads or necks,
Having their eyes plac'd on their shoulders, and
Their mouths amidst their breasts?

Diana   Ay, so indeed;   100
Though heels go upwards, an their feet should slip
They have no necks to break!

Doctor   Silence, sweet lady;
Pray give the gentleman leave to understand me.
The people through the whole world of Antipodes,
In outward feature, language and religion,
Resemble those to whom they are supposite.
They under Spain appear like Spaniards;
Under France, Frenchmen; under England, English,
To the exterior show – but in their manners,
Their carriage, and condition of life,   110
Extremely contrary. To come close to you:
What part o'th' world's Antipodes shall I now
Decipher to you, or would you travel to?

Peregrine   The furthest off.

Doctor   That is th'Antipodes of England.
The people there are contrary to us,
As thus: here, heaven be prais'd, the magistrates
Govern the people; there the people rule
The magistrates.

Diana   There's precious bribing then!

Joyless   You'll hold your peace.

Doctor   Nay, lady, 'tis by nature.
Here generally men govern the women –   120

Joyless   I would they could else!

Diana   You will hold your peace!

Doctor   But there the women overrule the men.
             If some men fail here in their power, some women
             Slip their holds there. As parents here and masters
             Command, there they obey the child and servant.

Diana   But pray, sir, is't by nature or by art
             That wives o'ersway their husbands there?

Doctor   By nature.

Diana   Then art's above nature, as they are under us.

Doctor   In brief, sir, all
             Degrees of people, both in sex and quality,   130
             Deport themselves in life and conversation
             Quite contrary to us.

Diana   Why then, the women
             Do get the men with child, and put the poor fools
             To grievous pain, I warrant you, in bearing.

Joyless   In to your chamber! Get you in, I charge you.

Doctor   By no means, as you tender your son's good.
             No, lady, no; that were to make men women
             And women men. But there the maids do woo
             The bachelors, and 'tis most probable
             The wives lie uppermost.

Diana   That is a trim,   140
             Upside down, Antipodean trick indeed!

Doctor   And then at christenings and gossips' feasts,
             A woman is not seen; the men do all
             The tittle-tattle duties, while the women
             Hunt, hawk and take their pleasure.

Peregrine   Ha' they good game, I pray, sir?

Doctor   Excellent;
             But by the contraries to ours, for where

We hawk at pheasant, partridge, mallard, heron,
With goshawk, tercel, falcon, lanneret,   149
Our hawks become their game, our game their hawks.
And so the like in hunting: there the deer
Pursue the hounds, and – which you may think strange –
I ha' seen one sheep worry a dozen foxes
By moonshine, in a morning before day.
They hunt train-scents with oxen, and plough with dogs.

Peregrine   [laughs] Hugh, hugh, hugh!

Diana   Are not their swans all black and ravens white?

Doctor   Yes, indeed are they, and their parrots teach
              Their mistresses to talk.

Diana   That's very strange.

Doctor   They keep their cats in cages,   160
              From mice that would devour them else; and birds
              Teach 'em to whistle and cry 'Beware the rats, Puss!'
              But these are frivolous nothings. I have known
              Great ladies ride great horses, run at tilt,
              At ring, races and hunting matches, while
              Their lords at home have painted, pawn'd their plate
              And jewels to feast their honourable servants.
              And there the merchants' wives do deal abroad
              Beyond seas, while their husbands cuckold them
              At home.

Diana   Then there are cuckolds, too, it seems,   170
              As well as here.

Joyless   Then you conclude here are!

Diana   By hearsay, sir. I am not wise enough
              To speak it on my knowledge yet.

Joyless   Not yet!

Doctor	Patience, good sir.
Peregrine	Hugh, hugh, hugh!
Doctor	What, do you laugh that there is cuckold-making
	In the Antipodes? I tell you, sir,
	It is not so abhorr'd here as 'tis held
	In reputation there. All your old men
	Do marry girls, and old women, boys,
	As generation were to be maintain'd 180
	Only by cuckold-making.
Joyless	Monstrous!
Doctor	Pray, your patience.
	There's no such honest men there in their world
	As are their lawyers. They give away
	Their practice, and t'enable 'em to do so,
	Being all handicrafts or labouring men,
	They work – poor hearts, full hard – in the vacations
	To give their law for nothing in the term times.
	No fees are taken, which makes their divines,
	Being generally covetous, the greatest wranglers
	In lawsuits of a kingdom. You have not there 190
	A gentleman in debt, though citizens
	Haunt them with cap in hand to take their wares
	On credit.
Diana	What fine sport would that be here now!
Doctor	All wit and mirth and good society
	Is there among the hirelings, clowns and tradesmen –
	And all their poets are puritans.
Diana	Ha' they poets?
Doctor	And players too; but they are all the sob'rest,
	Precisest people pick'd out of a nation.
Diana	I never saw a play.

Doctor	Lady, you shall.
Joyless	She shall not!
Doctor	She must, if you can hope for any cure. 200
	Be govern'd, sir; your jealousy will grow
	A worse disease than your son's madness else.
	You are content I take the course I told you of
	To cure the gentleman?
Joyless	I must be, sir.
Doctor	Say, Master Peregrine, will you travel now
	With me to the Antipodes, or has not
	The journey wearied you in the description?
Peregrine	No, I could hear you a whole fortnight, but
	Let's lose no time. Pray, talk on as we pass.
Doctor	First, sir, a health to auspicate our travels, 210
	And we'll away.
Peregrine	Gi' me't.
	[DOCTOR *offers wine-bowl to* PEREGRINE]

Enter BLAZE [*with a letter*]

	What's he? One sent,
	I fear, from my dead mother to make stop
	Of our intended voyage.
Doctor	No, sir. Drink.
Blaze	[*aside to* DOCTOR] My lord, sir, understands the
	course you're in
	By your letters, he tells me; and bad me gi' you
	This ring, which wants a finger here, he says.
Peregrine	We'll not be stay'd?
Doctor	No, sir, he brings me word
	The mariner calls away. The wind and tide

	Are fair; and they are ready to weigh anchor,
	Hoist sails and only stay for us. Pray drink, sir. 220

Peregrine   A health then to the willing winds and seas
            And all that steer towards th'Antipodes!   [*Drinks*]

Joyless   He has not drunk so deep a draught this twelvemonth.

Doctor   'Tis a deep draught indeed, and now 'tis down,
            And carries him down to the Antipodes!
            I mean but in a dream.

Joyless   Alas, I fear!
            See, he begins to sink.

Doctor   Trust to my skill.
            Pray take an arm, and see him in his cabin.
            Good lady, save my ring that's fallen there.

Diana   In sooth, a marvellous neat and costly one!   230

Blaze   [*aside*] So, so, the ring has found a finger.

Doctor   Come, sir, aboard, aboard, aboard, aboard!
                                  [*Exeunt all except* BLAZE]

Blaze   To bed, to bed, to bed! I know your voyage,
            And my dear lord's dear plot I understand,
            Whose ring hath pass'd here by your sleight of hand.
                                                          [*Exit*]

ACT 2, SCENE 1

[Enter] LETOY *[and]* DOCTOR

Letoy   Tonight, sayest thou, my Hughball?

Doctor   By all means:
And if your play takes to my expectation,
As I not doubt my potion works to yours,
Your fancy and my cure shall be cried up
Miraculous. Oh, you're the lord of fancy.

Letoy   I'm not ambitious of that title, sir.
Ages before the fancies were begot,
And shall beget still new to the world's end.
But are you confident o'your potion, doctor?   10
Sleeps the young man?

Doctor   Yes, and has slept these twelve hours,
After a thousand mile an hour outright
By sea and land, and shall awake anon
In the Antipodes.

Letoy   Well, sir, my actors
Are all in readiness; and, I think, all perfect
But one, that never will be perfect in a thing
He studies. Yet he makes such shifts *extempore*,
Knowing the purpose what he is to speak to,
That he moves mirth in me 'bove all the rest.
For I am none of those poetic furies   20
That threats the actor's life in a whole play
That adds a syllable or takes away.
If he can fribble through and move delight
In others, I am pleas'd.

Doctor It is that mimic fellow
Which your lordship but lately entertain'd.

Letoy The same.

Doctor He will be wondrous apt in my affair;
For I must take occasion to interchange
Discourse with him sometimes amidst their scenes,
T'inform my patient, my mad young traveller,
In divers matters.

Letoy Do – put him to't. I use't myself sometimes.

Doctor I know it is your way.

Letoy Well, to the business.
Hast wrought the jealous gentleman, old Joyless,
To suffer his wife to see our comedy?

Doctor She brings your ring, my lord, upon her finger –
And he brings her in's hand. I have instructed her
To spur his jealousy off o'the legs.

Letoy And I will help her in't.

Doctor The young distracted
Gentlewoman too, that's sick of her virginity,
Yet knows not what it is, and Blaze and's wife
Shall all be your guests tonight, and not alone
Spectators, but, as we will carry it, actors
To fill your comic scenes with double mirth.

Letoy Go fetch 'em then, while I prepare my actors.
Exit DOCTOR
Within there, ho!

1 (within) This is my beard and hair.

2 (within) My lord appointed it for my part.

3 (within) No.
This is for you; and this is yours, this grey one.

4 (*within*)	Where be the foils and targets for the women?
1 (*within*)	Here, can't you see?
Letoy	What a rude coil is there! But yet it pleases me.
1 (*within*)	You must not wear 50 That cloak and hat.
2 (*within*)	Who told you so? I must, In my first scene, and you must wear that robe.
Letoy	What a noise make those knaves! Come in, one of you.

Enter QUAILPIPE, *three Actors and* BYPLAY

[*To* QUAILPIPE] Are you the first that answers to that
    name?

Quailpipe	My lord.
Letoy	Why are not you ready yet?
Quailpipe	I am not to put on my shape before I have spoke the prologue. And for that, my lord, I yet want something.
Letoy	What, I pray, with your grave formality?
Quailpipe	I want my beaver shoes and leather cap 60 To speak the prologue in, which were appointed By your lordship's own direction.
Letoy	Well, sir, well – [*fetches them*] There they be for you. I must look to all.
Quailpipe	Certes, my lord, it is a most apt conceit, The comedy being the world turn'd upside down, That the presenter wear the capital beaver Upon his feet, and on his head shoe leather.

Letoy	Trouble not you your head with my conceit,
	But mind your part. Let me not see you act now
	In your scholastic way you brought to town wi'ye, 70
	With seesaw sack-a-down, like a sawyer.
	Nor in a comic scene play Hercules Furens,
	Tearing your throat to split the audients' ears.
	[*To another*] And you, sir, you had got a trick of late
	Of holding out your bum in a set speech,
	Your fingers fibulating on your breast
	As if your buttons or your band-strings were
	Helps to your memory. Let me see you in't
	No more, I charge you. [*To another*] No, nor you, sir, in
	That over-action of the legs I told you of, 80
	Your singles and your doubles, look you: thus –
	Like one o'th' dancing masters o'the Bear-garden.
	[*To another*] And when you have spoke, at end of every
	speech,
	Not minding the reply, you turn you round
	As tumblers do, when betwixt every feat
	They gather wind by firking up their breeches.
	I'll none of these absurdities in my house,
	But words and action married so together
	That shall strike harmony in the ears and eyes
	Of the severest, if judicious, critics. 90
Quailpipe	My lord, we are corrected.
Letoy	Go, be ready.
	[*Exeunt* QUAILPIPE *and the three Actors*]
	[*To* BYPLAY] But you, sir, are incorrigible, and
	Take licence to yourself to add unto
	Your parts your own free fancy, and sometimes
	To alter or diminish what the writer
	With care and skill compos'd. And when you are
	To speak to your co-actors in the scene,
	You hold interlocutions with the audients.

Byplay	That is a way, my lord, has been allow'd
	On elder stages to move mirth and laughter. 100
Letoy	Yes, in the days of Tarleton and Kemp,
	Before the stage was purg'd from barbarism
	And brought to the perfection it now shines with.
	Then fools and jesters spent their wits because
	The poets were wise enough to save their own
	For profitabler uses. Let that pass.
	Tonight I'll give thee leave to try thy wit
	In answering my doctor and his patient
	He brings along with him to our Antipodes.
Byplay	I heard of him, my lord. Blaze gave me light 110
	Of the mad patient, and that he never saw
	A play in's life. It will be possible
	For him to think he is in the Antipodes
	Indeed, when he is on the stage among us:
	When't has been thought by some that have their wits
	That all the players i'th' town were sunk past rising.
Letoy	Leave that, sir, to th'event. See all be ready,
	Your music, properties, and –
Byplay	All, my lord.
	Only we want a person for a mute.
Letoy	Blaze, when he comes, shall serve. Go in. *Exit* BYPLAY
	My guests, I hear, are coming. 121

Enter BLAZE, JOYLESS, DIANA, MARTHA [*and*] BARBARA

Blaze	My lord, I am become your honour's usher
	To these your guests. The worthy Master Joyless,
	With his fair wife and daughter-in-law.
Letoy	They're welcome,
	And you in the first place, sweet Mistress Joyless.
	You wear my ring, I see; you grace me in it.

Joyless	His ring? What ring? How came she by't?
Blaze	[*aside*] 'Twill work.
Letoy	I sent it as a pledge of my affection to you,
	For I before have seen you and do languish
	Until I shall enjoy your love.
Joyless	[*aside*] He courts her! 130
Letoy	Next, lady – you – I have a toy for you too.
Martha	My child shall thank you for it, when I have one.
	I take no joy in toys since I was married.
Letoy	Prettily answer'd. – I make you no stranger,
	Kind Mistress Blaze.
Barbara	[*aside*] Time was your honour us'd me strangely too;
	As you'll do these, I doubt not.
Letoy	Honest Blaze,
	Prithee go in; there is an actor wanting.
Blaze	Is there a part for me? How shall I study't?
Letoy	Thou shalt say nothing.
Blaze	Then if I do not act 140
	Nothing as well as the best of 'em, let me be hissed. *Exit*
Joyless	[*aside to* DIANA] I say restore the ring, and back with
	me.
Diana	To whom shall I restore it?
Joyless	To the lord that sent it.
Diana	Is he a lord? I always thought and heard
	I'th' country, lords were gallant creatures. He
	Looks like a thing not worth it. 'Tis not his;
	The doctor gave it me, and I will keep it.

Letoy	I use small verbal courtesy, Master Joyless,
	You see; but what I can in deed, I'll do.
	You know the purpose of your coming, and 150
	I can but give you welcome. If your son
	Shall receive ease in't, be the comfort yours,
	The credit of't my doctor's. You are sad.
Joyless	My lord, I would entreat we may return;
	I fear my wife's not well.
Letoy	Return? Pray slight not so my courtesy.
Diana	Besides, sir, I am well, and have a mind,
	A thankful one, to taste my lord's free bounty.
	I never saw a play and would be loath
	To lose my longing now.
Joyless	[*aside*] The air of London 160
	Hath tainted her obedience already;
	And should the play but touch the vices of it,
	She'd learn and practise 'em. – Let me beseech
	Your lordship's reacceptance of the un-
	Merited favour that she wears here, and
	Your leave for our departure.
Letoy	I will not
	Be so dishonour'd, nor become so ill
	A master of my house, to let a lady
	Leave it against her will, and from her longing.
	I will be plain wi' ye therefore. If your haste 170
	Must needs post you away, you may depart;
	She shall not, not till the morning, for mine honour.
Joyless	[*aside*] Indeed, 'tis a high point of honour in
	A lord to keep a private gentleman's wife
	From him.
Diana	I love this plain lord better than
	All the brave gallant ones that e'er I dreamt on.

Letoy   'Tis time we take our seats. So, if you'll stay,
               Come sit with us; if not, you know your way.   178

Joyless   [*aside*] Here are we fallen through the doctor's fingers
               Into the lord's hands. Fate, deliver us!   *Exeunt omnes*

ACT 2, SCENE 2

Enter, in sea gowns and caps, DOCTOR *and* PEREGRINE,
brought in a chair by two Sailors. Cloaks and hats brought in

Doctor   Now the last minute of his sleeping fit
               Determines. Raise him on his feet. So, so.
               Rest him upon mine arm. Remove that chair. –
               Welcome ashore, sir, in th'Antipodes.

Peregrine   Are we arriv'd so far?

Doctor   And on firm land.
               Sailors, you may return now to your ship. *Exeunt Sailors*

Peregrine   What worlds of lands and seas have I pass'd over,
               Neglecting to set down my observations!
               A thousand thousand things remarkable
               Have slipp'd my memory, as if all had been   10
               Mere shadowy phantasms or fantastic dreams.

Doctor   We'll write as we return, sir; and 'tis true
               You slept most part o'th' journey hitherward,
               The air was so somniferous. And 'twas well:
               You scap'd the calenture by't.

Peregrine   But how long do
               You think I slept?

Doctor   Eight months and some odd days,

Which was but as so many hours and minutes
Of one's own natural country sleep.

Peregrine   Eight months!

Doctor   'Twas nothing for so young a brain.
How think you? One of the seven Christian champions,
David by name, slept seven years in a leek bed.   21

Peregrine   I think I have read it in their famous history.

Doctor   But what chief thing of note now in our travels
Can you call presently to mind? Speak like a traveller.

Peregrine   I do remember – as we pass'd the verge
O'th' upper world, coming down, downhill –
The setting sun, then bidding them good night,
Came gliding easily down by us and struck
New day before us, lighting us our way;
But with such heat that, till he was got far   30
Before us, we even melted.

Doctor   [aside]   Well-wrought potion!
– Very well observ'd, sir.
But now we are come into a temperate clime,
Of equal composition of elements
With that of London, and as well agreeable
Unto our nature as you have found that air.

Peregrine   I never was at London.

Doctor   Cry you mercy.
This, sir, is anti-London. That's the Antipodes
To the grand city of our nation:
Just the same people, language and religion,   40
But contrary in manners, as I ha' told you.

Peregrine   I do remember that relation
As if you had but given it me this morning.

Doctor	Now cast your sea weeds off and don fresh garments.

        [*They*] *shift* [*their sea gowns and caps for cloaks and hats*]

                          Hautboys

        Hark, sir, their music.   [*They sit*]

Enter LETOY, JOYLESS, DIANA, MARTHA
[*and*] BARBARA *in masks, they sit at the other end of the stage*

Letoy	Here we may sit, and he not see us.

Doctor	[*to* PEREGRINE] Now see one of the natives of this country.

        Note his attire, his language and behaviour.

Enter QUAILPIPE [*as*] *Prologue*

Quailpipe	Our far-fetch'd title over lands and seas	
	Offers unto your view th'Antipodes.	50
	But what Antipodes now shall you see?	
	Even those that foot to foot 'gainst London be,	
	Because no traveller that knows that state	
	Shall say we personate or imitate	
	Them in our actions; for nothing can,	
	Almost, be spoke but some or other man	
	Takes it unto himself, and says the stuff,	
	If it be vicious or absurd enough,	
	Was woven upon his back. Far, far be all	
	That bring such prejudice mix'd with their gall.	60
	This play shall no satiric timist be	
	To tax or touch at either him or thee	
	That art notorious. 'Tis so far below	
	Things in our orb that do among us flow,	
	That no degree, from kaiser to the clown,	
	Shall say 'This vice or folly was mine own'.	

Letoy	This had been well now, if you had not dreamt	
	Too long upon your syllables. *Exit* QUAILPIPE	

Diana	The prologue call you this, my lord?

Barbara	'Tis my lord's reader, and as good a lad,	70
	Out of his function, as I would desire	
	To mix withal in civil conversation.	

Letoy   [*to* DIANA] Yes, lady, this was prologue to the play,
As this is to our sweet ensuing pleasures.   *Kisses* [*her*]

Joyless   [*aside*] Kissing indeed is prologue to a play
Compos'd by th' devil and acted by the Children
Of his Black Revels. May hell take ye for't!

Martha   Indeed, I am weary and would fain go home.

Barbara   Indeed, but you must stay and see the play.

Martha   The play? What play? It is no children's play,   80
Nor no child-getting play, pray, is it?

Barbara   You'll see anon. (*Flourish*) Oh, now the actors enter.

Enter two SERGEANTS, *with swords drawn,*
running before a GENTLEMAN

Gentleman   Why do you not your office, courteous friends?
Let me entreat you stay and take me with you.
Lay but your hands on me. I shall not rest
Until I be arrested. A sore shoulder-ache
Pains and torments me till your virtuous hands
Do clap or stroke it.

1 Sergeant   You shall pardon us.

2 Sergeant   And I beseech you pardon our intent,
Which was indeed to have arrested you.   90
But sooner shall the charter of the city
Be forfeited than varlets like ourselves
Shall wrong a gentleman's peace. So, fare you well, sir.
                                        Exeunt [SERGEANTS]

Gentleman   Oh, you're unkind.

Peregrine   Pray, what are those?

Doctor	Two catchpolls
	Run from a gentleman, it seems, that would
	Have been arrested.

Enter Old LADY *and* BYPLAY, *like a Servingman*

Lady	Yonder's your master.
	Go, take him you in hand, while I fetch breath.
Byplay	Oh, are you here? My lady and myself
	Have sought you sweetly –
Letoy	[*aside*] You and your lady,
	You should ha' said, puppy.
Byplay	For we heard you were 100
	To be arrested. Pray, sir, who has bail'd you?
	I wonder who of all your bold acquaintance
	That knows my lady durst bail off her husband.
Gentleman	Indeed, I was not touch'd.
Byplay	Have you not made
	An end by composition, and disburs'd
	Some of my lady's money for a peace
	That shall beget an open war upon you?
	Confess it if you have, for 'twill come out.
	She'll ha' you up, you know. I speak it for your good.
Gentleman	I know't, and I'll entreat my lady wife 110
	To mend thy wages t'other forty shillings
	A year for thy true care of me.
Lady	'Tis well, sir.
	But now – if thou hast impudence so much
	As face to face to speak unto a lady
	That is thy wife and supreme head – tell me
	At whose suit was it? Or upon what action?
	Debts I presume you have none, for who dares trust
	A lady's husband who is but a squire

	And under covert-barne? It is some trespass –
	Answer me not till I find out the truth. 120
Gentleman	The truth is –
Lady	Peace! How dar'st thou speak the truth
	Before thy wife! I'll find it out myself.
Diana	In truth, she handles him handsomely.
Joyless	Do you like it?
Diana	Yes, and such wives are worthy to be lik'd
	For giving good example.
Letoy	[*aside to* DIANA] Good! Hold up
	That humour by all means.
Lady	I think I ha' found it.
	There was a certain mercer sent you silks
	And cloth of gold to get his wife with child.
	You slighted her, and answer'd not his hopes,
	And now he lays to arrest you. Is't not so? 130
Gentleman	Indeed, my lady wife, 'tis so.
Lady	For shame!
	Be not ingrateful to that honest man,
	To take his wares and scorn to lie with his wife.
	Do't, I command you. What did I marry you for?
	The portion that you brought me was not so
	Abundant, though it were five thousand pounds, –
	Considering, too, the jointure that I made you –
	That you should disobey me.
Diana	It seems the husbands
	In the Antipodes bring portions, and
	The wives make jointures.
Joyless	Very well observ'd! 140
Diana	And wives, when they are old and past child-bearing,

	Allow their youthful husbands other women.
Letoy	Right. And old men give their young wives like licence.
Diana	That I like well. Why should not our old men Love their young wives as well?
Joyless	Would you have it so?
Letoy	Peace, Master Joyless, you are too loud. Good, still!
Byplay	Do as my lady bids. You got her woman With child at half these words.
Gentleman	Oh, but another's Wife is another thing. Far be it from A gentleman's thought to do so, having a wife 150 And handmaid of his own, that he loves better.
Byplay	There said you well; but take heed, I advise you, How you love your own wench or your own wife Better than other men's.
Diana	Good Antipodean counsel.
Lady	Go to that woman; if she prove with child, I'll take it as mine own.
Gentleman	Her husband would Do so, but from my house I may not stray.
Martha	If it be me your wife commends you to, You shall not need to stray from your own house. [*Stands*] I'll go home with you.
Barbara	Precious! What do you mean? 160 Pray keep your seat. You'll put the players out.
Joyless	Here's goodly stuff! She's in the Antipodes too.
Peregrine	And what are those? [*seeing* LETOY *and guests*]
Doctor	All Antipodeans.

Attend, good sir.

Enter Waiting WOMAN, *great-bellied*

Lady   [*to* GENTLEMAN] You know your charge; obey it.

Woman   What is his charge, or whom must he obey,
      Good madam, with your wild authority?
      You are his wife, 'tis true, and therein may,
      According to our law, rule and control him.
      But you must know withal, I am your servant
      And bound by the same law to govern you   170
      And be a stay to you in declining age,
      To curb and qualify your headstrong will,
      Which otherwise would ruin you. Moreover,
      Though you're his wife, I am a breeding mother
      Of a dear child of his, and therein claim
      More honour from him than you ought to challenge.

Lady   In sooth, she speaks but reason.

Gentleman   Pray, let's home then.

Woman   [*to* GENTLEMAN]
      You have something there to look to, one would think,
      If you had any care. How well you saw
      Your father at school today! And knowing how apt 180
      He is to play the truant.

Gentleman   But is he not
      Yet gone to school?

Woman   Stand by, and you shall see.

Enter three OLD MEN *with satchels, &c.*

All 3   [*singing and dancing*]
       Domine, domine duster,
        Three knaves in a cluster, &c.

Gentleman Oh, this is gallant pastime! Nay, come on,
      Is this your school? Was that your lesson, ha?

1 Old Man	Pray now, good son, indeed, indeed.
Gentleman	Indeed,
	You shall to school. [*To* BYPLAY] Away with him, and take
	Their wagships with him, the whole cluster of 'em.
2 Old Man	You shan't send us now, so you shan't. 190
3 Old Man	We be none of your father, so we bain't.
Gentleman	Away with 'em, I say; and tell their schoolmistress
	What truants they are, and bid her pay 'em soundly.
All 3	Oh, oh, oh!
Byplay	Come, come, ye gallows-clappers.
Diana	Alas, will nobody beg pardon for
	The poor old boys?
Doctor	Sir, gentle sir, a word with you.
	[*Whispers to* BYPLAY]
Byplay	To strangers, sir, I can be gentle.
Letoy	Good!
	Now mark that fellow; he speaks *extempore*.
Diana	'Extempore' call you him? He's a dogged fellow
	To the three poor old things there. Fie upon him! 200
Peregrine	Do men of such fair years here go to school?
Byplay	They would die dunces else.
Peregrine	Have you no young men scholars, sir, I pray,
	When we have beardless doctors?
Doctor	[*aside*] He has wip'd
	My lips! – You question very wisely, sir.
Byplay	So, sir, have we, and many reverend teachers,
	Grave counsellors at law, perfect statesmen,

	That never knew use of razor, which may live
	For want of wit to lose their offices.
	These were great scholars in their youth; but when 210
	Age grows upon men here, their learning wastes
	And so decays, that if they live until
	Threescore, their sons send them to school again.
	They'd die as speechless else as newborn children.

Peregrine   'Tis a wise nation; and the piety
             Of the young men most rare and commendable.
             Yet give me, as a stranger, leave to beg
             Their liberty this day; and what they lose by't,
             My father, when he goes to school, shall answer.

Joyless   [*aside*] I am abus'd on that side too.

Byplay   'Tis granted.   220
             Hold up your heads and thank the gentleman,
             Like scholars, with your heels now.

All 3   *Gratias, gratias, gratias.*   *Exeunt*

Diana   [*aside*] Well done, son Peregrine! –
             [*To* JOYLESS]   He's in's wits, I hope.

Joyless   If you lose yours the while, where's my advantage?

Diana   And trust me, 'twas well done too of Extempore
             To let the poor old children loose. And now
             I look well on him, he's a proper man.

Joyless   [*aside*] She'll fall in love with the actor and undo me.

Diana   Does not his lady love him, sweet my lord?   230

Letoy   Love? Yes, and lie with him, as her husband does
             With's maid. It is their law in the Antipodes.

Diana   But we have no such laws with us.

Joyless   Do you
             Approve of such a law?

Diana	No, not so much In this case, where the man and wife do lie With their inferior servants. But in the other, Where the old citizen would arrest the gallant That took his wares and would not lie with's wife, There it seems reasonable, very reasonable.
Joyless	Does it?
Diana	Make't your own case. You are an old man; 240 I love a gentleman; you give him rich presents To get me a child, because you cannot. Must not We look to have our bargain?
Joyless	Give me leave Now to be gone, my lord, though I leave her Behind me. She is mad and not my wife, And I may leave her.
Letoy	Come, you are mov'd, I see. I'll settle all; but first prevail with you To taste my wine and sweetmeats. The comedians Shall pause the while. This you must not deny me. 249 *Exeunt* [LETOY, MARTHA, DIANA *and* BARBARA]
Joyless	I must not live here always. That's my comfort. *Exit*
Peregrine	I thank you, sir, for the poor men's release. It was the first request that I have made Since I came in these confines.
Byplay	'Tis our custom To deny strangers nothing; yea, to offer Of anything we have that may be useful In courtesy to strangers. Will you therefore Be pleas'd to enter, sir, this habitation And take such viands, beverage and repose As may refresh you after tedious travels?

Doctor	Thou tak'st him right, for I am sure he's hungry.	260
Peregrine	All I have seen since my arrival are Wonders, but your humanity excels.	
Byplay	Virtue in the Antipodes only dwells.	[*Exeunt*]

ACT 3, SCENE 1

[Enter] LETOY, JOYLESS, DIANA, MARTHA *[and]* BARBARA

Letoy	Yet, Master Joyless, are you pleas'd? You see Here's nothing but fair play, and all above board.
Joyless	But it is late, and these long intermissions By banqueting and courtship 'twixt the acts Will keep back the catastrophe of your play Until the morning light.
Letoy	All shall be short.
Joyless	And then in midst of scenes You interrupt your actors, and tie them To lengthen time in silence, while you hold Discourse by th' by.
Letoy	Pox o'thy jealousy. 10 Because I give thy wife a look or word Sometimes! What if I kiss – thus; I'll not eat her.
Joyless	*[aside]* So, so, his banquet works with him.
Letoy	And for my actors, they shall speak or not speak As much, or more, or less, and when I please. It is my way of pleasure, and I'll use it. So, sit. They enter. *Flourish*

Enter LAWYER *and* POET

Lawyer	Your case is clear, I understand it fully And need no more instructions. This shall serve To firk your adversary from court to court. 20 If he stand out upon rebellious legs

	But till *octavus Michaelis* next,
	I'll bring him on submissive knees.
Diana	What's he?
Letoy	A lawyer, and his client there's a poet.
Diana	Goes law so torn, and poetry so brave?
Joyless	Will you but give the actors leave to speak
	They may have done the sooner!
Lawyer	Let me see.
	This is your bill of parcels?
Poet	Yes, of all
	My several wares, according to the rates
	Delivered unto my debitor.

Diana   Wares, does he say?

Letoy   Yes, poetry is good ware
In the Antipodes, though there be some ill payers,
As well as here; but law there rights the poets.

Lawyer   (*reads*) 'Delivered to and for the use of the right
    worshipful
Master Alderman Humblebee, as followeth:
Imprimis' – umh, I cannot read your hand:
Your character is bad, and your orthography
Much worse. Read it yourself, pray.

Diana   Do aldermen
Love poetry in Antipodean London?

Letoy   Better than ours do custards; but the worst
Paymasters living there – worse than our gallants –
Partly for want of money, partly wit.

Diana   Can aldermen want wit and money too?
That's wonderful.

Line numbers in right margin: 30 (at "Delivered unto my debitor."), 40 (at "Better than ours do custards; but the worst")

Poet   *Imprimis*, sir, here is
For three religious madrigals, to be sung
By th'holy vestals in Bridewell for the
Conversion of our city wives and daughters –
Ten groats a-piece: it was his own agreement.

Lawyer   'Tis very reasonable.

Poet   *Item*, twelve hymns
For the twelve sessions during his shrievalty,   50
Sung by the choir of Newgate in the praise
Of city clemency (for in that year
No guiltless person suffer'd by their judgement) –
Ten groats a-piece also.

Lawyer   So, now it rises.

Diana   Why speaks your poet so demurely?

Letoy   Oh,
'Tis a precise tone he has got among
The sober sisterhood.

Diana   Oh, I remember:
The doctor said poets were all puritans
In the Antipodes. But where's the doctor?
And where's your son, my Joyless?

Letoy   Do not mind him. 60

Poet   *Item*, a distich, graven in his thumb-ring,
Of all the wise speeches and sayings of all
His alder predecessors and his brethren
In two kings' reigns.

Lawyer   There was a curious piece.

Poet   Two pieces he promis'd to me for it.
Item, inscriptions, in his hall and parlour,
His gallery, and garden, round the walls,
Of his own public acts between the time

	He was a common councilman and shrieve:	
	One thousand lines put into wholesome verse.	70
Lawyer	Here's a sum towards indeed! A thousand verses?	
Poet	They come to, at the known rate of the city,	
	That is to say at forty pence the score,	
	Eight pounds, six shillings, eightpence.	
Lawyer	Well, sir, on.	
Poet	*Item*, an elegy for Mistress Alderwoman	
	Upon the death of one of her coach-mares	
	She priz'd above her daughter, being crooked –	
Diana	The more beast she.	
Martha	Ha, ha, ha!	
Barbara	Enough, enough, sweetheart.	
Martha	'Tis true, for I should weep for that poor daughter;	
	'Tis like she'll have no children. Pray now, look:	80
	Am not I crooked, too?	
Barbara	No, no. Sit down.	
Poet	*Item*, a love epistle for the aldermanikin	
	His son; and a book of the godly life and death	
	Of Mistress Katherine Stubbes, which I have turn'd	
	Into sweet metre for the virtuous youth	
	To woo an ancient lady widow with.	
Lawyer	Here's a large sum in all, for which I'll try	
	His strength in law till he *peccavi* cry,	
	When I shall sing, for all his present bigness,	
	Jamque opus exegi quod nec Jovis ira, nec ignis.	90
Diana	The lawyer speaks the poet's part.	
Letoy	He thinks	
	The more; the poets in th'Antipodes	

	Are slow of tongue but nimble with the pen.
Poet	The counsel and the comfort you have given me
	Requires a double fee. *Offers money*

Lawyer	Will you abuse me therefore?
	I take no fees, double nor single, I.
	Retain your money; you retain not me else.
	Away, away; you'll hinder other clients.

| Poet | Pray give me leave to send then to your wife. |

| Lawyer | Not so much as a posy for her thimble,   100 |
| | For fear I spoil your cause. |

| Poet | You've warn'd me, sir.   *Exit* |

| Diana | What a poor honest lawyer's this! |

| Letoy | They are all |
| | So in th'Antipodes. |

Enter a spruce young CAPTAIN

| Lawyer | You're welcome, captain. |
| | In your two causes I have done my best. |

| Captain | And what's the issue, pray, sir? |

| Lawyer | Truly, sir, |
| | Our best course is not to proceed to trial. |

| Captain | Your reason? I shall then recover nothing. |

Lawyer	Yes, more by composition than the court
	Can lawfully adjudge you, as I have labour'd;
	And, sir, my course is, where I can compound 110
	A difference, I'll not toss nor bandy it
	Into the hazard of a judgement.

| Diana | Still |
| | An honest lawyer, and though poor, no marvel. |

Letoy	A kiss for thy conceit.	*[Kisses her]*

Joyless [*aside*]   A sweet occasion!

Captain How have you done, sir?

Lawyer   First, you understand
Your several actions, and your adversaries:
The first, a battery against a coachman
That beat you sorely.

Diana   What hard-hearted fellow
Could beat so spruce a gentleman, and a captain?

Captain By this fair hilt, he did, sir, and so bruis'd   120
My arms, so crush'd my ribs and stitch'd my sides
That I have had no heart to draw my sword since.
And shall I put it up, and not his purse
Be made to pay for't?

Lawyer   It is up already, sir,
If you can be advis'd; observe, I pray.
Your other action's 'gainst your feathermaker,
And that of trespass, for th'incessant trouble
He puts you to by importunate requests
To pay him no money, but take longer day.

Captain Against all human reason, for although   130
I have bought feathers of him these four years
And never paid him a penny, yet he duns me
So desperately to keep my money still
As if I ow'd him nothing; he haunts and breaks my sleeps!
I swear, sir, by the motion of this I wear now,
                              shakes [his head]
I have had twenty better feathers of him,
And as ill paid for. Yet still he duns me to
Forbear my payment and to take longer day,
More than at first! I ha' not said my prayers
In mine own lodging, sir, this twelvemonth's day   140

For sight or thought of him; and how can you
Compound this action, or the other of
That ruffian coachman that durst lift a hand
'Gainst a commander?

Lawyer   Very easily, thus:
The coachman's poor, and scarce his twelvemonth's wages,
Though't be five marks a year, will satisfy.

Captain   Pray name no sum in marks; I have had too many
Of's marks already.

Lawyer   So you owe the other
A debt of twenty pound, the coachman now
Shall for your satisfaction beat you out   150
Of debt.

Captain   Beat me again?

Lawyer   No, sir, he shall beat
For you your featherman, till he take his money.

Captain   So I'll be satisfied, and help him to
More customers of my rank.

Lawyer   Leave it to me, then.
It shall be by posterity repeaten
That soldiers ought not to be dunned or beaten.
Away, and keep your money.

Captain   Thank you, sir.   [*Exit*]

Diana   An honest lawyer still! How he considers
The weak estate of a young gentleman
At arms.

                        Enter BUFF WOMAN

                        But who comes here? A woman?   160

Letoy   Yes, that has taken up the newest fashion
Of the town militasters.

Diana	Is it buff,
	Or calfskin, trow? She looks as she could beat
	Out a whole tavern garrison before her
	Of – mill-tasters, call you 'em? If her husband
	Be an old, jealous man now, and can please her
	No better than most ancient husbands can,

LAWYER reads on papers

	I warrant she makes herself good upon him.
Joyless	'Tis very good; the play begins to please me. 169
Buff Woman	[*to* LAWYER] I wait to speak w' ye, sir, but must I stand
	Your const'ring and piercing of your scribblings?
Lawyer	Cry mercy, lady.
Diana	'Lady' does he call her?
Lawyer	Thus far I have proceeded in your cause
	I'th' marshal's court.
Buff Woman	But shall I have the combat?
Lawyer	Pray observe
	The passages of my proceedings, and
	The pros and contras in the windings, workings
	And carriage of the cause.
Buff Woman	Fah on your passages,
	Your windy workings and your fizzlings at
	The bar. Come me to th' point. Is it decreed 180
	A combat?
Lawyer	Well, it is; and here's your order.
Buff Woman	Now thou hast spoken like a lawyer,
	And here's thy fee.
Lawyer	By no means, gentle lady.

Buff Woman	Take it, or I will beat thy carcass thinner Than thou hast worn thy gown here.
Lawyer	Pardon me.
Buff Woman	Must I then take you in hand?
Lawyer	[*accepts fee*] Hold, hold! I take it.
Diana	Alas, poor man! He will take money yet Rather than blows; and so far he agrees With our rich lawyers, that sometimes give blows, And shrewd ones, for their money.
Buff Woman	Now victory 190 Afford me, Fate, or bravely let me die. *Exit*
Letoy	Very well acted, that.
Diana	Goes she to fight now?
Letoy	You shall see that anon.

Enter a BEGGAR *and a* GALLANT

Diana	What's here, what's here? A courtier, or some gallant, practising The beggar's trade, who teaches him, I think.
Letoy	You're something near the subject.
Beggar	Sir, excuse me. I have From time to time supplied you, without hope Or purpose to receive least retribution From you; no, not so much as thanks or bare Acknowledgement of the free benefits 200 I have conferr'd upon you.
Gallant	Yet, good uncle –
Beggar	Yet do you now, when that my present store Responds not my occasions, seek to oppress me

With vain petitionary breath for what I may not
Give without fear of dangerous detriment?

Diana   In what a phrase the ragged orator
Displays himself!

Letoy   The beggars are the most
Absolute courtiers in th'Antipodes.

Gallant   If not a piece, yet spare me half a piece
For goodness sake, good sir. Did you but know   210
My instant want, and to what virtuous use
I would distribute it, I know you would not
Hold back your charity.

Diana   And how feelingly
He begs. Then, as the beggars are the best
Courtiers, it seems the courtiers are best beggars
In the Antipodes. How contrary in all
Are they to us!

Beggar   Pray, to what virtuous uses
Would you put money to now, if you had it?

Gallant   I would bestow a crown in ballads,
Love pamphlets and such poetical rarities   220
To send down to my lady grandmother.
She's very old, you know, and given much
To contemplation. I know she'll send me for 'em
In puddings, bacon, souse and pot-butter,
Enough to keep my chamber all this winter.
So shall I save my father's whole allowance
To lay upon my back, and not be forc'd
To shift out from my study for my victuals.

Diana   Belike he is some student.

Beggar   There's a crown.

Gallant   I would bestow another crown in hobby-   230

Horses and rattles for my grandfather,
Whose legs and hearing fail him very much;
Then, to preserve his sight, a Jack-a-Lent
In a green sarcenet suit. He'll make my father
To send me one of scarlet, or he'll cry
His eyes out for't.

Diana   Oh, politic young student.

Beggar   I have but just a fee left for my lawyer;
If he exact not that, I'll give it thee.

Diana   [*to* BEGGAR] He'll take no fee – that's sure enough,
          young man –
Of beggars, I know that.

Letoy   You are deceiv'd.   240

Diana   [*to* BEGGAR] I'll speak to him myself else, to remit it.

Joyless   You will not, sure. Will you turn actor, too?
Pray do, be put in for a share amongst 'em!

Diana   How must I be put in?

Joyless   The players will quickly
Show you, if you perform your part; perhaps
They may want one to act the whore amongst 'em.

Letoy   Fie, Master Joyless, you're too foul.

Joyless   My lord,
She is too fair, it seems, in your opinion,
For me; therefore, if you can find it lawful,
Keep her. I will be gone.

Letoy   Now, I protest,   250
Sit, and sit civilly, till the play be done!
I'll lock thee up else, as I am true Letoy.

Joyless   Nay. I ha' done.   *Whistles 'Fortune my foe'*

Lawyer	Give me my fee; I cannot hear you else.
Beggar	Sir, I am poor, and all I get is at The hands of charitable givers. Pray, sir –
Lawyer	You understand me, sir. Your cause is to be Pleaded today, or you are quite o'erthrown in't.

The judge by this time is about to sit.   259

Keep fast your money and forgo your wit.   *Exit*

Beggar	Then I must follow and entreat him to it;

Poor men in law must not disdain to do it.   *Exit*

Gallant	Do it, then. I'll follow you and hear the cause. *Exit*
Diana	True Antipodeans still; for as with us The gallants follow lawyers, and the beggars them, The lawyer here is follow'd by the beggar, While the gentleman follows him.
Letoy	The moral is, the lawyers here prove beggars, And beggars only thrive by going to law.
Diana	How takes the lawyers, then, the beggars' money, 270 And none else by their wills?
Letoy	They send it all Up to our lawyers, to stop their mouths That curse poor clients that are put upon 'em *In forma pauperis.*
Diana	In truth, most charitable; But sure that money's lost by th' way sometimes. Yet, sweet my lord, whom do these beggars beg of That they can get aforehand so for law? Who are their benefactors?
Letoy	Usurers, usurers.
Diana	Then they have usurers in th'Antipodes too?

Letoy	Yes, usury goes round the world, and will do 280
	Till the general conversion of the Jews.

Diana But ours are not so charitable, I fear.
Who be their usurers?

Letoy   Soldiers and courtiers chiefly,
And some that pass for grave and pious churchmen.

Diana How finely contrary they're still to ours!

Letoy [*calls*] Why do you not enter? What, are you asleep?

Enter BYPLAY

Byplay My lord, the mad young gentleman –

Joyless   What of him?

Byplay He has got into our tiring-house amongst us
And ta'en a strict survey of all our properties:
Our statues and our images of gods;   290
Our planets and our constellations;
Our giants, monsters, furies, beasts and bugbears;
Our helmets, shields and visors; hairs and beards;
Our pasteboard marchpanes and our wooden pies –

Letoy Sirrah, be brief. Be not you now as long
In telling what he saw as he surveying.

Byplay Whether he thought 'twas some enchanted castle,
Or temple, hung and pil'd with monuments
Of uncouth and of various aspects,
I dive not to his thoughts. Wonder he did   300
Awhile it seem'd, but yet undaunted stood;
When on the sudden, with thrice-knightly force
And thrice-thrice-puissant arm he snatcheth down
The sword and shield that I play'd Bevis with,
Rusheth amongst the foresaid properties,
Kills monster after monster, takes the puppets

Prisoners, knocks down the Cyclops, tumbles all
Our jiggumbobs and trinkets to the wall.
Spying at last the crown and royal robes
I'th' upper wardrobe, next to which by chance   310
The devils' visors hung and their flame-painted
Skin coats, those he remov'd with greater fury;
And, having cut the infernal ugly faces
All into mammocks, with a reverent hand
He takes the imperial diadem and crowns
Himself King of the Antipodes, and believes
He has justly gain'd the kingdom by his conquest.

Letoy   Let him enjoy his fancy.

Byplay   Doctor Hughball
Hath sooth'd him in it, so that nothing can
Be said against it. He begins to govern   320
With purpose to reduce the manners of
This country to his own. He's constituted
The doctor his chief officer, whose secretary
I am to be. You'll see a court well order'd.

Letoy   I see th'event already, by the aim
The doctor takes. Proceed you with your play,
And let him see it in what state he pleases.

Byplay   I go, my lord.   *Exit*
                       LETOY *whispers with* BARBARA

Diana   Trust me, this same Extempore
(I know not's tother name) pleases me better
For absolute action than all the rest.   330

Joyless   You were best beg him of his lord.

Diana   Say you so?
He's busy, or I'd move him.

Letoy   [*to* BARBARA]   Prithee do so,

Good Mistress Blaze. – (*To* MARTHA) Go with her,
   gentle lady.
Do as she bids you. You shall get a child by't.

Martha	I'll do as anybody bids me for a child.

Joyless	Diana, yet be wise; bear not the name
	Of sober chastity to play the beast in.

Diana   Think not yourself, nor make yourself, a beast
        Before you are one; and when you appear so,   339
        Then thank yourself. Your jealousy durst not trust me
        Behind you in the country, and, since I'm here,
        I'll see and know and follow th' fashion; if
        It be to cuckold you, I cannot help it.

Joyless   I now could wish my son had been as far
        In the Antipodes as he thinks himself
        Ere I had run this hazard.

Letoy   [*to* BARBARA]   You're instructed.

Barbara And I'll perform't, I warrant you, my lord.
                Exeunt BARBARA [*and*] MARTHA

Diana   Why should you wish so? Had you rather lose your son
        Than please your wife? You show your love both ways!

Letoy	Now what's the matter?

Joyless   Nothing, nothing.

Letoy   Sit.   350
        The actors enter.

Flourish. Enter BYPLAY [*as*] *the governor, Macebearer,*
SWORDBEARER, OFFICER. *The mace and sword laid*
on the table, the governor sits

Diana	What's he, a king?

Letoy   No, 'tis the city governor,
And the chief judge within their corporation.

Joyless	Here's a city like to be well govern'd then!

Enter PEREGRINE *and* DOCTOR

Letoy	Yonder's a king. Do you know him?
Diana	'Tis your son, My Joyless. Now you're pleas'd.
Joyless	Would you were pleas'd To cease your housewif'ry in spinning out The play at length thus.
Doctor	Here, sir, you shall see A point of justice handled.
Byplay	Officer.
Officer	My lord.
Byplay	Call the defendant and the plaintiff in. 360
Swordbearer	Their counsel and their witnesses.
Byplay	How now! How long ha' you been free o'th' pointmakers, Good Master hilt-and-scabbard carrier (Which is in my hands now)? Do you give order For counsel and for witnesses in a cause Fit for my hearing, or for me to judge, haw? I must be rul'd and circumscrib'd by lawyers, Must I, and witnesses, haw? No, you shall know I can give judgement, be it right or wrong, Without their needless proving and defending! 370 So bid the lawyers go and shake their ears, If they have any, and the witnesses Preserve their breath to prophesy of dry summers. Bring me the plaintiff and defendant only, But the defendant first. I will not hear Any complaint before I understand What the defendant can say for himself. [*Exit* OFFICER]

Peregrine	I have not known such downright equity.
	If he proceeds as he begins, I'll grace him.

Enter GENTLEMAN *and* OFFICER

Byplay	Now, sir, are you the plaintiff or defendant, haw?	380
Gentleman	Both, as the case requires, my lord.	
Byplay	I cannot	
	Hear two at once. Speak first as you're defendant.	
Gentleman	Mine adversary doth complain –	
Byplay	I will hear no	
	Complaint. I say speak your defence.	
Gentleman	For silks	
	And stuffs receiv'd by me –	
Byplay	A mercer is he, haw?	
Gentleman	Yes, my good lord. He doth not now complain –	
Byplay	That I like well.	
Gentleman	For money nor for wares	
	Again; but he complains –	
Byplay	Complains again?	
	Do you double with me, haw?	
Gentleman	In his wife's cause.	
Byplay	Of his wife, does he, haw? That I must confess	390
	Is many a good man's case. You may proceed.	
Gentleman	In money I tender him double satisfaction,	
	With his own wares again unblemish'd, undishonour'd.	
Byplay	That is, unworn, unpawned.	
Diana	What an odd,	
	Jeering judge is this?	

Gentleman	But unto me They were deliver'd, upon this condition That I should satisfy his wife.
Byplay	He'll have Your body for her then, unless I empt My breast of mercy to appease her for you. Call in the plaintiff! *Exit* OFFICER [*To* GENTLEMAN] Sir, stand you aside. 400
Diana	Oh, 'tis the flinching gentleman that broke With the kind citizen's wife. I hope the judge Will make him an example.

Enter CITIZEN *and* OFFICER

Byplay	Come you forwards; Yet nearer, man. I know my face is terrible, And that a citizen had rather lose His debt than that a judge should truly know His dealings with a gentleman. Yet speak, Repeat without thy shopbook now, and without Fear it may rise in judgement here against thee; What is thy full demand? What satisfaction 410 Requirest thou of this gentleman?
Citizen	An't please you, sir –
Swordbearer	Sir? You forget yourself.
Byplay	'Twas well said, swordbearer; Thou know'st thy place, which is to show correction.
Citizen	My lord, an't please you, if it like your honour –
Byplay	La! An intelligent citizen, and may grow In time himself to sit in place of worship.
Citizen	I ask no satisfaction of the gentleman But to content my wife. What her demand is, 'Tis best known to herself: please her, please me –

	An't please you, sir; my lord, an't like your honour. 420
	But before he has given her satisfaction
	I may not fall my suit nor draw my action.

Byplay You may not?

Citizen   No, alack-a-day, I may not;
Nor find content nor peace at home, an't please you,
My lord (an't like your honour, I would say).
An't please you, what's a tradesman that
Has a fair wife without his wife, an't please you?
And she without content is no wife. Considering
We tradesmen live by gentlemen, an't please you,
And our wives drive a half-trade with us, if the
  gentlemen   430
Break with our wives, our wives are no wives to us,
And we but broken tradesmen, an't please you,
An't like your honour, my good lord, an't please you.

Byplay You argue honestly.

Citizen   Yet gentlemen –
Alack-a-day, an't please you, an't like your honour –
Will not consider our necessities,
And our desire in general through the city
To have our sons all gentlemen like them.

Byplay Nor, though a gentleman consume
His whole estate among ye, yet his son   440
May live t'inherit it?

Citizen   Right, right, an't please you,
Your honour, my good lord, an't please you.

Byplay   Well,
This has so little to be said against it
That you say nothing. Gentleman, it seems
You're obstinate and will stand out –

Gentleman   My lord,
Rather than not to stand out with all men's wives

Except mine own, I'll yield me into prison.

Citizen Alack-a-day!

Diana   If our young gentlemen
Were like those of th'Antipodes, what decay
Of trade would here be, and how full the prisons!   450

Gentleman I offer him any other satisfaction;
His wares again, or money twice the value.

Byplay That's from the point.

Citizen   Ay, ay, alack-a-day,
Nor do I sue to have him up in prison.
Alack-a-day, what good – good gentleman –
Can I get by his body?

Byplay   Peace. I should
Now give my sentence; and for your contempt –
Which is a great one, such as if let pass
Unpunish'd may spread forth a dangerous
Example to the breach of city custom,   460
By gentlemen's neglect of tradesmen's wives –
I should, I say, for this contempt commit you
Prisoner from sight of any other woman
Until you give this man's wife satisfaction,
And she release you; justice so would have it.
But as I am a citizen by nature
(For education made it so), I'll use
Urbanity in your behalf towards you.
And as I am a gentleman by calling
(For so my place must have it), I'll perform   470
For you the office of a gentleman
Towards his wife. I therefore order thus:
[*to* GENTLEMAN] That you bring me the wares here
    into court –
I have a chest shall hold 'em as mine own;
[*to* CITIZEN] And you send me your wife – I'll satisfy
    her

	Myself. I'll do't, and set all straight and right.	
	Justice is blind, but judges have their sight.	
Diana	And feeling too, in the Antipodes.	
	Ha'n't they, my lord?	
Joyless	What's that to you, my lady?	
Prompter	(*within*) 'Dismiss the court.'	480
Letoy	'Dismiss the court'; cannot you hear the prompter?	
	Ha' you lost your ears, judge?	
Byplay	No. [*To* OFFICER] Dismiss the court.	

Embrace you, friends, and to shun further strife,
See you send me your stuff, and you your wife.

[*Exeunt* OFFICER, CITIZEN *and* GENTLEMAN]

Peregrine	Most admirable justice.

[BYPLAY *removes his robes*]

Diana	'Protest, Extempore play'd the judge! And I
	Knew him not all this while.
Joyless	What oversight
	Was there!
Diana	He is a properer man, methinks,
	Now than he was before; sure I shall love him.
Joyless	Sure, sure you shall not, shall you?
Diana	And I warrant, 490

By his judgement speech e'en now, he loves a woman
Well; for he said, if you noted him, that he
Would satisfy the citizen's wife himself.
Methinks a gentlewoman might please him better.

Joyless	How dare you talk so!

BYPLAY *kneels, and kisses* PEREGRINE'*s hand*

Diana	What's he a-doing now, trow?
Peregrine	Kneel down again. Give me a sword, somebody.
Letoy	The King's about to knight him.

Byplay
                          Let me pray
Your majesty be pleas'd yet to withhold
That undeserved honour till you first
Vouchsafe to grace the city with your presence.   500
Accept one of our hall feasts, and a freedom,
And freely use our purse for what great sums
Your majesty will please.

Diana
                                 What subjects there are
In the Antipodes!

Letoy
                     None in the world so loving.

Peregrine
Give me a sword, I say. Must I call thrice?

Letoy
No, no, take mine, my liege.

Peregrine
                         Yours? What are you?

Doctor
A loyal lord; one of your subjects too.

Peregrine
He may be loyal; he's a wondrous plain one.

Joyless
Prithee, Diana, yet let's slip away   509
Now, while he's busy.

Diana
                       But where's your daughter-in-law?

Joyless
Gone home, I warrant you, with Mistress Blaze.
Let them be our example.

Diana
                    You are cozen'd.

Joyless
You're an impudent whore!

Diana
                        I know not what I may be
Made by your jealousy.

Peregrine	[*Throws down* LETOY'*s sword*] I'll none o'this. Give me that princely weapon. [*Points at sword of office*]
Letoy	Give it him.
Swordbearer	[*aside to* LETOY] It is a property, you know, my lord, No blade, but a rich scabbard with a lath in't.
Letoy	So is the sword of Justice, for aught he knows.
Peregrine	[*fails to draw sword from scabbard*] It is enchanted.
Byplay	Yet on me let it fall, Since 'tis your highness' will, scabbard and all. 520
Peregrine	Rise up, our trusty well-beloved knight.
Byplay	Let me find favour in your gracious sight To taste a banquet now, which is prepar'd, And shall be by your followers quickly shar'd.
Peregrine	My followers? Where are they?
Letoy	[*calls*] Come, sirs, quickly.

Enter 5 or 6 Courtiers

Peregrine	'Tis well. Lead on the way. [*Exeunt* PEREGRINE *and Courtiers*]
Diana	And must not we Go to the banquet too?
Letoy	He must not see You yet. I have provided otherwise For both you in my chamber, and from thence We'll at a window see the rest o'th' play; 530 Or if you needs, sir, will stay here, you may.
Joyless	[*aside*] Was ever man betray'd thus into torment? *Exeunt*

ACT 4, SCENE 1

Enter DOCTOR *and* PEREGRINE

Doctor	Now, sir, be pleas'd to cloud your princely raiment
	With this disguise. [PEREGRINE] *puts on a cloak and hat*
	Great kings have done the like
	To make discovery of passages
	Among the people; thus you shall perceive
	What to approve and what correct among 'em.
Peregrine	And so I'll cherish or severely punish.

Enter an OLD WOMAN, *reading [a handbill]*;
to her a young MAID *[with a book]*

Doctor	Stand close, sir, and observe.
Old Woman	[*reads*] 'Royal pastime in a great match between the
	tanners and the butchers, six dogs of a side to play
	single at the game bear for fifty pound, and a ten- 10
	pound supper for their dogs and themselves. Also
	you shall see two ten-dog courses at the great bear.'
Maid	Fie, granny, fie! Can no persuasions,
	Threat'nings nor blows prevail, but you'll persist
	In these profane and diabolical courses?
	To follow bear-baitings, when you can scarce
	Spell out their bills with spectacles?
Old Woman	What though
	My sight be gone beyond the reach of spectacles
	In any print but this, and though I cannot –
	No, no, I cannot – read your meditations, 20
	strikes down MAID's *book*
	Yet I can see the royal game play'd over and over,

	And tell which dog does best, without my spectacles.
	And though I could not, yet I love the noise;
	The noise revives me, and the Bear-garden scent
	Refresheth much my smelling.

Maid   Let me entreat you
Forbear such beastly pastimes; they're satanical.

Old Woman   Take heed, child, what you say. 'Tis the King's game.

Peregrine   What is my game?

Doctor   Bear-baiting, sir, she means.

Old Woman   'A bear's a princely beast and one side venison',
Writ a good author once. You yet want years   30
And are with baubles pleas'd; I'll see the bears.   *Exit*

Maid   And I must bear with it. She's full of wine
And for the present wilful; but in due
Season I'll humble her. But we are all
Too subject to infirmity.

Enter a young GENTLEMAN *and an old* SERVINGMAN

Gentleman   Boy. Boy.

Servingman   Sir.

Gentleman   Here, take my cloak.

Peregrine   Boy, did he say?

Doctor   Yes, sir. Old servants are
But boys to masters, be they ne'er so young.

Gentleman   'Tis heavy and I sweat.

Servingman   Take mine and keep
You warm then. I'll wear yours.   [*They exchange cloaks*]

Gentleman   Out, you varlet!   40
Dost thou obscure it as thou meant'st to pawn it?

	Is this a cloak unworthy of the light? Publish it, sirrah. Oh, presumptuous slave, Display it on one arm! Oh, ignorance!
Servingman	Pray load your ass yourself as you would have it.

Gentleman	Nay, prithee, be not angry.
	          [Arranges cloak on SERVINGMAN's *arm]*
	               Thus; and now
	Be sure you bear't at no such distance but
	As't may be known appendix to this book.

Peregrine	This custom I have seen with us.
Doctor	Yes, but It was deriv'd from the Antipodes.

50

Maid	*[aside]* It is a dainty creature, and my blood Rebels against the spirit. I must speak to him.
Servingman	Sir, here's a gentlewoman makes towards you.
Gentleman	Me? She's deceiv'd. I am not for her mowing.
Maid	Fair sir, may you vouchsafe my company?

Gentleman	No; truly I am none of those you look for.
	The way is broad enough.
	            [MAID takes hold of GENTLEMAN]*
	          Unhand me, pray you.

Maid	Pray, sir, be kinder to a lass that loves you.
Gentleman	Some such there are, but I am none of those.
Maid	Come, this is but a copy of your countenance. I ha' known you better than you think I do.

60

Gentleman	What ha' you known me for?
Maid	I knew you once For half a piece, I take it.

Gentleman	You are deceiv'd The whole breadth of your nose. I scorn it!
Maid	Come, be not coy, but send away your servant And let me gi' you a pint of wine.
Gentleman	Pray keep Your courtesy. I can bestow the wine Upon myself, if I were so dispos'd To drink in taverns. Fah!
Maid	Let me bestow't Upon you at your lodging then, and there 70 Be civilly merry.
Gentleman	Which if you do My wife shall thank you for it. But your better Course is to seek one fitter for your turn. You'll lose your aim in me, and I befriend you To tell you so.
Maid	Gip, gaffer shotten, fagh! Take that for your coy counsel. *Kicks* [GENTLEMAN]
Gentleman	Help! Oh, help!
Servingman	What mean you, gentlewoman?
Maid	That to you, sir. *Kicks* [SERVINGMAN]
Gentleman	Oh murder, murder!
Servingman	Peace, good master, And come away. Some cowardly jade, I warrant, That durst not strike a woman.

Enter CONSTABLE *and* WATCH

Constable	What's the matter? 80
Servingman	[*to* MAID] But an we were your match –

Watch	What would you do?
	Come, come, afore the constable, now: if
	You were her match, what would you do, sir?
Maid	Do?
	They have done too much already, sir. (*Weeps*) A virgin
	Shall not pass shortly for these streetwalkers,
	If some judicious order be not taken.
Gentleman	Hear me the truth.
Constable	Sir, speak to your companions.
	I have a wife and daughters and am bound
	By hourly precepts to hear women first,
	Be't truth or no truth. Therefore, virgin, speak, 90
	And fear no bugbears. I will do thee justice.
Maid	Sir, they assail'd me and with violent hands,
	When words could not prevail, they would have drawn
	me
	Aside unto their lust, till I cried murder.
Gentleman	'Protest, sir, as I am a gentleman
	And as my man's a man, she beat us both
	Till I cried murder.
Servingman	That's the woeful truth on't.
Constable	You are a party and no witness, sir.
	Besides you're two, and one is easier
	To be believ'd. Moreover, as you have the odds 100
	In number, what were justice if it should not support
	The weaker side? Away with them to the Counter.
Peregrine	Call you this justice?
Doctor	In th'Antipodes.
Peregrine	Here's much to be reform'd. Young man, thy virtue
	Hath won my favour. Go, thou art at large.

[GENTLEMAN *hesitates*]

Doctor	[*aside*] Be gone.
Gentleman	[*aside*] He puts me out; my part is now To bribe the constable.
Doctor	[*aside*] No matter, go. *Exeunt* GENTLEMAN *and* SERVINGMAN
Peregrine	[*to* CONSTABLE] And you, sir, take that sober- seeming wanton And clap her up till I hear better of her. I'll strip you of your office and your ears else. 110
Doctor	At first show mercy.
Peregrine	They are an ignorant nation, And have my pity mingled with correction. And, therefore, damsel – for you are the first Offender I have noted here and this Your first offence, for aught I know –
Maid	Yes, truly.
Doctor	[*aside to* MAID] That was well said.
Peregrine	Go, and transgress no more; And, as you find my mercy sweet, see that You be not cruel to your grandmother When she returns from bear-baiting.
Doctor	[*aside*] So, all be gone. *Exeunt* [*all but* PEREGRINE *and* DOCTOR]

Enter BUFF WOMAN, *her head and face bleeding,*
and many Women as from a prize

Peregrine	And what are these? 120
Doctor	A woman fencer that has play'd a prize, It seems, with loss of blood.

Peregrine	It doth amaze me.
	They pass over [the stage, and exeunt]
	What can her husband be when she's a fencer?
Doctor	He keeps a school and teacheth needlework,
	Or some such arts which we call womanish.
Peregrine	'Tis most miraculous and wonderful.
Man-Scold	(*within*) Rogues, varlets, harlots, ha' you done your worst,
	Or would you drown me? Would you take my life?
Women	(*within*) Duck him again. Duck him again.
Peregrine	What noise is this?
Doctor	Some man, it seems, that's duck'd for scolding.
Peregrine	A man, for scolding?
Doctor	You shall see.

Enter WOMEN *and* MAN-SCOLD

1 Woman	So, so;	131
	Enough, enough. He will be quiet now.	
Man-Scold	How know you that, you devil-ridden witch, you?	
	How, quiet? Why quiet? Has not the law pass'd on me,	
	Over and over me, and must I be quiet?	
1 Woman	Will you incur the law the second time?	
Man-Scold	The law's the river, is't? Yes, 'tis a river	
	Through which great men and cunning wade or swim;	
	But mean and ignorant must drown in't. No,	
	You hags and hellhounds, witches, bitches, all	140
	That were the law, the judge and executioners,	
	To my vexation, I hope to see	
	More flames about your ears than all the water	
	You cast me in can quench.	

2 Woman	In with him again,
	He calls us names!

Man-Scold	No, no – I charge ye, no!

Was ever harmless creature so abus'd?
To be drench'd under water, to learn dumbness
Amongst the fishes, as I were forbidden
To use the natural members I was born with,
And of them all the chief that man takes pleasure in,
The tongue! Oh me, accursed wretch!   *Weeps*

Peregrine   Is this a man? 151
I ask not by his beard but by his tears.

1 Woman   This shower will spend the fury of his tongue,
And so the tempest's over.

2 Woman   I am sorry for't;
I would have had him duck'd once more.
But somebody will shortly raise the storm
In him again, I hope, for us to make
More holiday-sport of him.
                    Exeunt [WOMEN *and* MAN-SCOLD]

Peregrine   Sure these are dreams,
Nothing but dreams.

Doctor   No, doubtless we are awake, sir.

Peregrine   Can men and women be so contrary   160
In all that we hold proper to each sex?

Doctor   [*aside*] I'm glad he takes a taste of sense in that yet.

Peregrine   'Twill ask long time and study to reduce
Their manners to our government.

Doctor   These are
Low things and easy to be qualified.
But see, sir, here come courtiers; note their manners.

Enter a COURTIER [*counting his money*]

1 Courtier	This was three shillings yesterday. How now!
	All gone but this? Sixpence for leather soles
	To my new green silk stockings and a groat
	My ordinary in pompions bak'd with onions. 170

Peregrine   Do such eat pompions?

Doctor   Yes, and clowns musk-melons.

[*Enter* 2 COURTIER *unseen by the first*]

1 Courtier   Threepence I lost at ninepins – but I got
Six tokens towards that at pigeon-holes.
'Snails, where's the rest? Is my poke bottom broke?

2 Courtier   What, Jack! A pox o'ertake thee now! How dost?
                                                    Kicks [*him*]

1 Courtier   What with a vengeance ail'st? Dost think my breech
Is made of bell metal? Take that!   *Box o'th' ear*

2 Courtier   In earnest?

1 Courtier   Yes, till more comes.   [*Seizes his hair*]

2 Courtier   Pox rot your hold. Let go my lock. D'ye think
You're currying of your father's horse again?   180

1 Courtier   I'll teach you to abuse a man behind
Was troubled too much afore.   *They buffet*

Enter 3 COURTIER

3 Courtier   Hey, there boys, there.
Good boys are good boys still. There, Will. There, Jack.
                    [1 COURTIER *knocks down* 2]
Not a blow, now he's down.

1 Courtier   'Twere base. I scorn't.

2 Courtier   There's as proud fall as stand, in court or city.

3 Courtier	That's well said, Will. Troth, I commend you both. How fell you out? I hope in no great anger.
2 Courtier	For mine own part, I vow I was in jest.
1 Courtier	But I have told you twice and once, Will, jest not With me behind. I never could endure, 190 Not of a boy, to put up things behind, And that my tutor knew – I had been a scholar else! Besides, you know my sword was nock'd i'th' fashion, Just here behind, for my back-guard and all, And yet you would do't! I had as lief you would take a knife –
3 Courtier	Come, come, You're friends. Shake hands. I'll give you half a dozen At the next alehouse to set all right and straight, And a new song, a dainty one. Here 'tis. *[Produces] a [printed] ballad*
1 Courtier	Oh, thou art happy that canst read. 200 I would buy ballads too, had I thy learning.
3 Courtier	Come; we burn daylight and the ale may sour. *Exeunt* [COURTIERS]
Peregrine	Call you these courtiers? They are rude silken clowns, As coarse within as watermen or carmen.
Doctor	Then look on these. Here are of those conditions.

Enter CARMAN *and* WATERMAN

Waterman	Sir, I am your servant.
Carman	I am much oblig'd, Sir, by the plenteous favours your humanity And noble virtue have conferr'd upon me, To answer with my service your deservings.
Waterman	You speak what I should say. Be therefore pleas'd 210

T'unload and lay the weight of your commands
Upon my care to serve you.

Carman   Still your courtesies,
Like waves of a spring tide, o'erflow the banks
Of your abundant store, and from your channel
Or stream of fair affections you cast forth
Those sweet refreshings on me, that were else
But sterile earth, which cause a gratitude
To grow upon me, humble, yet ambitious
In my devoir to do you best of service.

Waterman   I shall no more extend my utmost labour   220
With oar and sail to gain the livelihood
Of wife and children than to set ashore
You and your faithful honourers at the haven
Of your best wishes.

Carman   Sir, I am no less
Ambitious to be made the happy means,
With whip and whistle, to draw up or drive
All your detractors to the gallows.

                    Enter SEDAN-MAN

Waterman   See,
Our noble friend.

Sedan-man   Right happily encounter'd.
I am the just admirer of your virtues.

Carman &
  Waterman   We are in all your servants.

Sedan-man   I was in quest   230
Of such elect society to spend
A dinner time withal.

Carman &
  Waterman   Sir, we are for you.

Sedan-man	Three are the golden number in a tavern:
	And at the next of best, with the best meat
	And wine the house affords, if you so please,
	We will be competently merry. I
	Have receiv'd lately letters from beyond seas
	Importing much of the occurrences
	And passages of foreign states. The knowledge
	Of all I shall impart to you.

Waterman   And I   240
Have all the new advertisements from both
Our universities of what has pass'd
The most remarkably of late.

Carman   And from the court I have the news at full
Of all that was observable this progress.

Peregrine   From court?

Doctor   Yes, sir. They know not there they have
A new king here at home.

Sedan-man   'Tis excellent!
We want but now the news-collecting gallant
To fetch his dinner and materials
For his this week's dispatches.

Waterman   I dare think   250

The meat and news being hot upon the table
He'll smell his way to't.

Sedan-man   Please you to know yours, sir?

Carman   Sir, after you.

Sedan-man   Excuse me.

Waterman   By no means, sir.

Carman   Sweet sir, lead on.

Sedan-man	It shall be as your servant
	Then, to prepare your dinner. [*Exit*]
Waterman	Pardon me.
Carman	In sooth, I'll follow you.
Waterman	Yet 'tis my obedience.

Exit [WATERMAN, *then* CARMAN]

Peregrine Are these but labouring men and t'other courtiers?

Doctor 'Tis common here, sir, for your watermen
To write most learnedly when your courtier
Has scarce ability to read.

Peregrine   Before I reign   260
A month among them they shall change their notes,
Or I'll ordain a course to change their coats.
I shall have much to do in reformation.

Doctor Patience and counsel will go through it, sir.

Peregrine What if I crav'd – a counsel from New England?
The old will spare me none.

Doctor [*aside*]   Is this man mad?
My cure goes fairly on. – Do you marvel that
Poor men outshine the courtiers? Look you, sir:

*These persons pass over the stage in couples,
according as he describes them*

A sick man giving counsel to a physician;
And there's a puritan tradesman teaching a   270
Great traveller to lie; that ballad-woman
Gives light to the most learned antiquary
In all the kingdom.

*Ballad-
woman*   Buy new ballads, come.

Doctor   A natural fool, there, giving grave instructions
                 T'a lord ambassador; that's a schismatic
                 Teaching a scrivener to keep his ears;
                 A parish clerk, there, gives the rudiments
                 Of military discipline to a general;
                 And there's a basket-maker confuting Bellarmine.

Peregrine   Will you make me mad?

Doctor   We are sail'd, I hope,   280
                 Beyond the line of madness.

Enter BYPLAY, *like a statesman,* [*and*] *three or four* PROJECTORS
with bundles of papers

                                        Now, sir, see
                 A statesman, studious for the commonwealth,
                 Solicited by projectors of the country.

Byplay   Your projects are all good; I like them well,
                 Especially these two: this for th'increase of wool,
                 And this for the destroying of mice. They're good,
                 And grounded on great reason. – As for yours,
                 For putting down the infinite use of jacks,
                 Whereby the education of young children
                 In turning spits is greatly hinder'd,   290
                 It may be looked into. – And yours against
                 The multiplicity of pocket watches,
                 Whereby much neighbourly familiarity,
                 By asking, 'What d'ye guess it is o'clock?',
                 Is lost, when every puny clerk can carry
                 The time o'th' day in's breeches: this, and these,
                 Hereafter may be look'd into. For present,
                 This, for the increase of wool, that is to say,
                 By flaying of live horses and new covering them
                 With sheepskins, I do like exceedingly –   300
                 And this, for keeping of tame owls in cities
                 To kill up rats and mice, whereby all cats

	May be destroy'd, as an especial means
	To prevent witchcraft and contagion.
Peregrine	Here's a wise business!
Projector	Will your honour now
	Be pleas'd to take into consideration
	The poor men's suits for briefs to get relief,
	By common charity throughout the kingdom,
	Towards recovery of their lost estates?
Byplay	What are they? Let me hear.
Projector	First, here's a gamester that sold house and land
	To the known value of five thousand pounds
	And by misfortune of the dice lost all,
	To his extreme undoing, having neither
	A wife or child to succour him.
Byplay	A bachelor?
Projector	Yes, my good lord.
Byplay	And young and healthful?
Projector	Yes.
Byplay	Alas, 'tis lamentable! He deserves
	Much pity.
Peregrine	How's this?
Doctor	Observe him further, pray, sir.
Projector	Then, here's a bawd of sixty-odd years' standing.
Byplay	How old was she when she set up?
Projector	But four
	And twenty, my good lord. She was both ware
	And merchant, flesh and butcher, as they say,
	For the first twelve years of her housekeeping.
	She's now upon fourscore and has made markets

310

320

Of twice four thousand choice virginities
And twice their number of indifferent gear
(No riff-raff was she ever known to cope for).
Her life is certified here by the justices
Adjacent to her dwelling –

Byplay   She is decay'd?   329

Projector Quite trade-fallen, my good lord, now in her dotage
And desperately undone by riot.

Byplay   'Las, good woman.

Projector She has consum'd in prodigal feasts and fiddlers
And lavish lendings to debauch'd comrades
That suck'd her purse, in jewels, plate and money,
To the full value of six thousand pounds.

Byplay She shall have a collection and deserves it.

Peregrine 'Tis monstrous, this.

Projector   Then here are divers more,
Of panders, cheaters, house and highway robbers,
That have got great estates in youth and strength
And wasted all as fast in wine and harlots,   340
Till age o'ertook 'em and disabled them
For getting more.

Byplay   For such the law provides
Relief within those counties where they practis'd.

Peregrine Ha! What, for thieves?

Doctor   Yes. Their law punisheth
The robb'd and not the thief, for surer warning
And the more safe prevention. I have seen
Folks whipp'd for losing of their goods and money
And the pickpockets cherish'd.

Byplay   The weal public,
As it severely punisheth their neglect

	Undone by fire-ruins, shipwreck and the like	350
	With whips, with brands and loss of careless ears,	
	Imprisonment, banishment and sometimes death,	
	And carefully maintaineth houses of correction	
	For decay'd scholars and maim'd soldiers,	
	So doth it find relief and almshouses	
	For such as liv'd by rapine and by cozenage.	

Peregrine   Still worse and worse! Abominable! Horrid!

Projector   Yet here is one, my lord, 'bove all the rest,
Whose services have generally been known,
Though now he be a spectacle of pity.   360

Byplay   Who's that?

Projector   The captain of the cutpurses, my lord,
That was the best at's art that ever was,
Is fallen to great decay by the dead palsy
In both his hands and craves a large collection.

Byplay   I'll get it him.

Peregrine   You shall not get it him!
Do you provide whips, brands and ordain death
For men that suffer under fire or shipwreck
The loss of all their honest-gotten wealth,
And find relief for cheaters, bawds and thieves?
I'll hang ye all.

Byplay   Mercy, great King.

Omnes   Oh, mercy!   370

Byplay   Let not our ignorance suffer in your wrath
Before we understand your highness' laws.
We went by custom and the warrant which
We had in your late predecessor's reign.
But let us know your pleasure, you shall find
The state and commonwealth in all obedient

	To alter custom, law, religion, all,	
	To be conformable to your commands.	
Peregrine	'Tis a fair protestation – and my mercy	
	Meets your submission. See you merit it	380
	In your conformity.	
Byplay	Great sir, we shall.	

LETOY, DIANA [*and*] JOYLESS *appear above*

	In sign whereof we lacerate these papers	
	And lay our necks beneath your kingly feet.	
Peregrine	Stand up. You have our favour. [*Exeunt* PROJECTORS]	
Diana	And mine, too!	
	Never was such an actor as Extempore!	
Joyless	You were best to fly out of the window to him.	
Diana	Methinks I am even light enough to do it.	
Joyless	I could find in my heart to quoit thee at him.	
Diana	So he would catch me in his arms I car'd not.	
Letoy	Peace, both of you, or you'll spoil all.	
Byplay	[*to* PEREGRINE] Your grace	390
	Abounds – abounds – your grace – I say, abounds –	
Letoy	Pox o'your mumbling chops. Is your brain dry?	
	Do you pump?	
Diana	He has done much, my lord, and may	
	Hold out a little.	
Letoy	Would you could hold your peace	
	So long.	
Diana	Do you sneap me too, my lord?	
Joyless	Ha, ha, ha!	
Letoy	Blockhead!	

Joyless	[*aside*] I hope his hotter zeal to's actors Will drive out my wife's love heat.
Diana	I Had no need to come hither to be sneap'd.
Letoy	Hoyday! The rest will all be lost. We now Give over the play and do all by *extempore* 400 For your son's good, to soothe him into's wits. If you'll mar all, you may. [*Aside to* BYPLAY] Come nearer, cockscomb. Ha' you forgotten, puppy, my instructions Touching his subjects and his marriage?
Byplay	[*aside*] I have all now, my lord. [*Flourish*]
Peregrine	What voice was that?
Byplay	A voice out of the clouds that doth applaud Your highness' welcome to your subjects' loves.
Letoy	So, now he's in. [*To* JOYLESS *and* DIANA] Sit still, I must go down And set out things in order. *Exit*

Byplay	A voice that doth inform me of the tidings 410
	Spread through your kingdom of your great arrival
	And of the general joy your people bring
	To celebrate the welcome of their king. *Shouts within*
	Hark how the country shouts with joyful votes,
	Rending the air with music of their throats.
	                    Drum and trumpets
	Hark how the soldier with his martial noise
	Threatens your foes, to fill your crown with joys.
	                    Hautboys
	Hark how the city with loud harmony
	Chants a free welcome to your majesty. *Soft music*
	Hark how the court prepares your grace to meet 420
	With solemn music, state and beauty sweet.

The soft music playing, enter by two and two divers courtiers; MARTHA
after them like a queen, between two boys in robes, her train borne up by
BARBARA. *All the lords kneel and kiss* PEREGRINE'*s hand.*
MARTHA *approaching, he starts back, but is drawn on by* BYPLAY
and the DOCTOR. LETOY *enters and mingles with the rest*
and seems to instruct them all

Diana	Oh, here's a stately show! Look, Master Joyless:
	Your daughter-in-law presented like a queen
	Unto your son. I warrant now he'll love her.
Joyless	A queen?
Diana	Yes, yes, and Mistress Blaze is made
	The mother of her maids – if she have any;
	Perhaps the Antipodean court has none.
	See, see, with what a majesty he receives 'em.

Song

Health, wealth and joy our wishes bring
All in a welcome to our king.   430
   May no delight be found,
   Wherewith he be not crown'd.
   Apollo with the Muses,
   Who arts divine infuses,
With their choice garlands deck his head.
Love and the graces make his bed,
 And to crown all, let Hymen to his side
Plant a delicious, chaste and fruitful bride.

Byplay	Now, sir, be happy in a marriage choice
	That shall secure your title of a king. 440
	See, sir, your state presents to you the daughter,
	The only child and heir apparent of
	Our late deposed and deceased sovereign,
	Who with his dying breath bequeath'd her to you.
Peregrine	A crown secures not an unlawful marriage.
	I have a wife already.

Doctor	No. You had, sir, But she's deceas'd.
Peregrine	How know you that?
Doctor	By sure advertisement; and that her fleeting spirit Is flown into and animates this princess.
Peregrine	Indeed she's wondrous like her.
Doctor	Be not slack 450 T'embrace and kiss her, sir.

PEREGRINE *kisses her and retires*

Martha	He kisses sweetly; And that is more than e'er my husband did. But more belongs than kissing to child-getting; And he's so like my husband, if you note him, That I shall but lose time and wishes by him. No, no, I'll none of him.
Barbara	I'll warrant you he shall fulfil your wishes.
Martha	Oh, but try him you first and then tell me.
Barbara	There's a new way, indeed, to choose a husband! [*Aside*] Yet 'twere a good one to bar fool-getting. 460
Doctor	Why do you stand aloof, sir?
Peregrine	Mandeville writes Of people near the Antipodes call'd Gadlibriens, Where on the wedding night the husband hires Another man to couple with his bride To clear the dangerous passage of a maidenhead.
Doctor	[*aside*] 'Slid, he falls back again to Mandeville madness.
Peregrine	She may be of that serpentine generation That stings oft-times to death, as Mandeville writes.
Doctor	She's no Gadlibrien, sir, upon my knowledge. You may as safely lodge with her as with 470

	A maid of our own nation. Besides,
	You shall have ample counsel. For the present
	Receive her and entreat her to your chapel.
Byplay	For safety of your kingdom you must do it.

Hautboys. Exeunt in state as LETOY *directs.* LETOY *remains*

Letoy	So, so, so, so; this yet may prove a cure –
Diana	[*above*] See, my lord now is acting by himself.
Letoy	And Letoy's wit cried up triumphant, ho!
	Come, Master Joyless and your wife, come down
	Quickly; your parts are next.

[*Exeunt above* JOYLESS *and* DIANA]

I had almost

Forgot to send my chaplain after them.   480
You, *domine*, where are you?

Enter QUAILPIPE *in a fantastical shape*

Quailpipe	Here, my lord.
Letoy	What, in that shape?
Quailpipe	'Tis for my part, my lord,
	Which is not all perform'd.
Letoy	It is, sir, and the play, for this time. We
	Have other work in hand.
Quailpipe	Then have you lost
	Action – I dare be bold to speak it! – that
	Most of my coat could hardly imitate.
Letoy	Go, shift your coat, sir, or for expedition
	Cover it with your own, due to your function.
	Follies as well as vices may be hid so; 490
	Your virtue is the same. Dispatch, and do
	As Doctor Hughball shall direct you. Go.

Exit QUAILPIPE

Enter JOYLESS *and* DIANA

Now, Master Joyless, do you note the progress
And the fair issue likely to ensue
In your son's cure? Observe the doctor's art.
First, he has shifted your son's known disease
Of madness into folly and has wrought him
As far short of a competent reason as
He was of late beyond it. As a man
Infected by some foul disease is drawn   500
By physic into an anatomy
Before flesh fit for health can grow to rear him,
So is a madman made a fool before
Art can take hold of him to wind him up
Into his proper centre, or the medium
From which he flew beyond himself. The doctor
Assures me now, by what he has collected
As well from learned authors as his practice,
That his much troubled and confused brain
Will, by the real knowledge of a woman,   510
Now opportunely ta'en, be by degrees
Settled and rectified, with the helps beside
Of rest and diet, which he'll administer.

Diana   But 'tis the real knowledge of the woman –
             Carnal, I think you mean – that carries it?

Letoy   Right, right.

Diana   Nay, right or wrong, I could even wish,
             If he were not my husband's son, the doctor
             Had made myself his recipe, to be the means
             Of such a cure.

Joyless   How, how?

Diana   Perhaps that course might cure your madness too   520
             Of jealousy – and set all right on all sides.
             [To LETOY] Sure, if I could but make him such a fool
             He would forgo his madness and be brought

To Christian sense again.

Joyless   Heaven grant me patience
And send us to my country home again!

Diana   Besides, the young man's wife's as mad as he.
What wise work will they make!

Letoy   The better, fear't not.
Bab Blaze shall give her counsel, and the youth
Will give her royal satisfaction
Now, in this kingly humour. – [*Aside to* DIANA] I have
    a way   530
To cure your husband's jealousy myself.

Diana   [*aside*] Then I am friends again; even now I was not,
When you sneap'd me, my lord.

Letoy   [*aside to* DIANA]   That you must pardon. –
Come, Master Joyless. The new-married pair
Are towards bed by this time. We'll not trouble them
But keep a house-side to ourselves. Your lodging
Is decently appointed.

Joyless   Sure your lordship
Means not to make your house our prison?

Letoy   By
My lordship but I will, for this one night.
See, sir, the keys are in my hand. You're up,   540
As I am true Letoy. Consider, sir,
The strict necessity that ties you to't
As you expect a cure upon your son.
Come, lady, see your chamber.

Diana   I do wait
Upon your lordship.

Joyless   [*aside*]   I both wait and watch;
Never was man so master'd by his match.   *Exeunt omnes*

ACT 5, SCENE 1

[Enter] JOYLESS *with a light in his hand*

Joyless   Diana! Ho! Where are you? She is lost.

[Finds doors are locked]

Here is no further passage. All's made fast.
This was the bawdy way by which she scap'd
My narrow watching. Have you privy posterns
Behind the hangings in your strangers' chambers?
She's lost from me forever! Why then seek I?
Oh my dull eyes, to let her slip so from ye,
To let her have her lustful will upon me!
Is this the hospitality of lords?
Why rather if he did intend my shame   10
And her dishonour did he not betray me
From her out of his house, to travail in
The bare suspicion of their filthiness,
But hold me a nose witness to its rankness?
No! This is sure the lordlier way and makes
The act more glorious in my sufferings. *[Kneels]* Oh!
May my hot curses on their melting pleasures
Cement them so together in their lust
That they may never part, but grow one monster.

Enter BARBARA

Barbara   *[aside]* Good gentleman, he is at his prayers now   20
For his mad son's good night-work with his bride. –
Well fare your heart, sir; you have pray'd to purpose,
But not all night, I hope. – Yet sure he has;
He looks so wild for lack of sleep. – You're happy, sir.
Your prayers are heard, no doubt, for I'm persuaded
You have a child got you tonight.

Joyless   Is't gone
            So far, do you think?

Barbara   I cannot say how far.
            Not fathom-deep, I think, but to the scantling
            Of a child-getting, I dare well imagine.
            For which, as you have pray'd, forget not, sir,   30
            To thank the lord o'th' house.

Joyless   For getting me
            A child? Why, I am none of his great lordship's tenants,
            Nor of his followers, to keep his bastards.
                                        [*Barbara offers to leave*]
            Pray stay a little.

Barbara   I should go tell my lord
            The news. He longs to know how things do pass.

Joyless   Tell him I take it well, and thank him.
            I did before despair of children, I.
            But I'll go wi' ye and thank him.

Barbara   [*aside*]   Sure his joy
            Has madded him. Here's more work for the doctor!

Joyless   But tell me first: [*draws a dagger*]
                  were you their bawd that speak this?

Barbara   What mean you with that dagger?   41

Joyless   Nothing. I
            But play with't. Did you see the passages
            Of things? I ask, were you their bawd?

Barbara   Their bawd?
            I trust she is no bawd that sees and helps,
            If need require, an ignorant lawful pair
            To do their best.

Joyless   Lords' actions all are lawful!
            And how? And how?

Barbara	[*aside*] These old folks love to hear. – I'll tell you, sir – and yet I will not neither.
Joyless	Nay, prithee, out with't.
Barbara	Sir, they went to bed –
Joyless	To bed! Well, on.
Barbara	On? They were off, sir, yet; 50 And yet a good while after. They were both So simple that they knew not what nor how, For she's, sir, a pure maid.
Joyless	Who dost thou speak of?
Barbara	I'll speak no more, 'less you can look more tamely.
Joyless	Go, bring me to 'em, then. Bawd, will you go? [*Goads her with dagger*]
Barbara	Ah! –

Enter BYPLAY *and holds* JOYLESS

Byplay	What ail you, sir? Why bawd? Whose bawd is she?
Joyless	Your lord's bawd and my wife's.
Byplay	You are jealous mad. Suppose your wife be missing at your chamber And my lord, too, at his, they may be honest. If not, what's that to her, or you, I pray, 60 Here in my lord's own house?
Joyless	Brave, brave and monstrous!
Byplay	She has not seen them. I heard all your talk. The child she intimated is your grandchild In *posse*, sir, and of your son's begetting.
Barbara	Ay, I'll be sworn I meant and said so too!

Joyless   Where is my wife?

Byplay   I can give no account.
            If she be with my lord I dare not trouble 'em,
            Nor must you offer at it. No, nor stab yourself –
                              BYPLAY *takes away his dagger*
            But come with me. I'll counsel or at least
            Govern you better. She may be, perhaps,   70
            About the bride-chamber to hear some sport,
            For you can make her none, 'las, good old man, –

Joyless   I'm most insufferably abus'd.

Byplay   – unless
            The killing of yourself may do't, and that
            I would forbear, because perhaps 'twould please her.

Joyless   If fire or water, poison, cord or steel
            Or any means be found to do it, I'll do it;
            Not to please her, but rid me of my torment.

Byplay   I have more care and charge of you than so.
                              Exeunt JOYLESS *and* BYPLAY

Barbara   What an old desperate man is this, to make   80
            Away yourself for fear of being a cuckold!
            If every man that is, or that but knows
            Himself to be, o'th' order should do so,
            How many desolate widows would here be!
            They are not all of that mind. Here's my husband.

                    Enter BLAZE *with a habit in his hand*

Blaze   Bab! Art thou here?

Barbara   Look well. How think'st thou, Tony?
            Hast not thou neither slept tonight?

Blaze   Yes, yes.
            I lay with the butler. Who was thy bedfellow?

Barbara	You know I was appointed to sit up.
Blaze	Yes, with the doctor in the bride-chamber. 90 But had you two no waggery, ha?
Barbara	Why, how now, Tony?
Blaze	Nay, facks, I am not jealous. Thou knowest I was cur'd long since and how. I jealous? I an ass. A man shan't ask His wife shortly how such a gentleman does, Or how such a gentleman did, or which did best, But she must think him jealous.
Barbara	You need not; for If I were now to die on't, nor the doctor Nor I came in a bed tonight. I mean Within a bed.
Blaze	Within, or without, or over, 100 Or under. I have no time to think o'such poor things.
Barbara	What's that thou carriest, Tony?
Blaze	Oho, Bab! This is a shape.
Barbara	A shape? What shape, I prithee, Tony?
Blaze	Thou'lt see me in't anon but shalt not know me From the stark'st fool i'th' town. And I must dance Naked in't, Bab.
Barbara	Will here be dancing, Tony?
Blaze	Yes, Bab. My lord gave order for't last night. It should ha' been i'th' play, but because that Was broke off he will ha 't today.
Barbara	Oh, Tony, I did not see thee act i'th' play.

Blaze	Oh, but	110
	I did though, Bab: two mutes.	

Barbara   What, in those breeches?

Blaze   Fie, fool! Thou understand'st not what a mute is.
             A mute is a dumb speaker in the play.

Barbara   Dumb speaker? That's a bull! Thou wert the bull,
             Then, in the play? Would I had seen thee roar.

Blaze   That's a bull too, as wise as you are, Bab.
             A mute is one that acteth speakingly
             And yet says nothing. I did two of them:
             The sage man-midwife and the basket-maker.

Barbara	Well, Tony, I will see thee in this thing,	120
	An 'tis a pretty thing.	

Blaze   Prithee, good Bab,
             Come in and help me on with't in our tiring-house
             And help the gentlemen, my fellow dancers,
             And thou shalt then see all our things and all
             Our properties and practice to the music.

Barbara	Oh, Tony, come. I long to be at that. *Exeunt*

ACT 5, SCENE 2

[*Enter*] LETOY *and* DIANA.
A table set forth, covered with treasure

Diana   My lord, your strength and violence prevail not.
             There is a providence above my virtue
             That guards me from the fury of your lust.

Letoy   Yet, yet, I prithee, yield. Is it my person
             That thou despisest? See, here's wealthy treasure,

Jewels that Cleopatra would have left
Her Marcus for.

Diana   My lord, 'tis possible
That she who leaves a husband may be bought
Out of a second friendship.

Letoy   Had stout Tarquin
Made such an offer he had done no rape,   10
For Lucrece had consented, sav'd her own
And all those lives that follow'd in her cause.

Diana   Yet then she had been a loser.

Letoy   Wouldst have gold?
Mammon nor Pluto's self should overbid me,
For I'd give all. First, let me rain a shower
To outvie that which o'erwhelm'd Danaë;
And after that another. A full river
Shall from my chests perpetually flow
Into thy store.

Diana   I have not much lov'd wealth,
But have not loath'd the sight of it till now   20
That you have soil'd it with that foul opinion
Of being the price of virtue. Though the metal
Be pure and innocent in itself, such use
Of it is odious, indeed damnable,
Both to the seller and the purchaser.
Pity it should be so abus'd. It bears
A stamp upon't, which but to clip is treason.
'Tis ill us'd there where law the life controls;
Worse, where 'tis made a salary for souls.

Letoy   Deny'st thou wealth? Wilt thou have pleasure then,   30
Given and ta'en freely without all condition?
I'll give thee such as shall, if not exceed,
Be at the least comparative with those

Which Jupiter got the demigods with – and
Juno was mad she miss'd.

Diana   My lord, you may
Gloss o'er and gild the vice which you call pleasure
With god-like attributes, when it is at best
A sensuality so far below
Dishonourable that it is mere beastly,
Which reason ought to abhor; and I detest it   40
More than your former hated offers.

Letoy   Lastly,
Wilt thou have honour? I'll come closer to thee,
For now the flames of love grow higher in me,
And I must perish in them or enjoy thee.
Suppose I find by power, or law, or both,
A means to make thee mine, by freeing
Thee from thy present husband.

Diana   Hold, stay there.
Now, should ye utter volumes of persuasions,
Lay the whole world of riches, pleasures, honours
Before me in full grant, that one last word   50
'Husband', and from your own mouth spoke, confutes
And vilifies even all. The very name
Of husband, rightly weigh'd and well remember'd,
Without more law or discipline, is enough
To govern womankind in due obedience,
Master all loose affections and remove
Those idols which too much too many love,
And you have set before me to beguile
Me of the faith I owe him. But remember
You grant I have a husband; urge no more.   60
I seek his love. 'Tis fit he loves no whore.

Letoy   [aside] This is not yet the way. – You have seen, lady,
My ardent love, which you do seem to slight,
Though to my death, pretending zeal to your husband.

My person nor my proffers are so despicable
But that they might, had I not vow'd affection
Entirely to yourself, have met with th'embraces
Of greater persons, no less fair, that can
Too, if they please, put on formality
And talk in as divine a strain as you.   70
This is not earnest! Make my word but good
Now with a smile, I'll give thee a thousand pound.
Look o'my face. Come! Prithee, look and laugh not.
Yes, laugh, an dar'st. Dimple this cheek a little;
I'll nip it else.

Diana   I pray forbear, my lord.
I'm past a child and will be made no wanton.

Letoy   How can this be? So young, so vigorous
And so devoted to an old man's bed!

Diana   That is already answer'd. He's my husband.
You are old too, my lord.

Letoy   Yes, but of better mettle.   80
A jealous old man too, whose disposition
Of injury to beauty and young blood
Cannot but kindle fire of just revenge
In you, if you be woman, to requite
With your own pleasure his unnatural spite.
You cannot be worse to him than he thinks you,
Considering all the open scorns and jeers
You cast upon him, to a flat defiance;
Then the affronts I gave to choke his anger;
And lastly your stol'n absence from his chamber.   90
All which confirms – we have as good as told him –
That he's a cuckold. Yet you trifle time
As 'twere not worth the doing.

Diana   Are you a lord?
Dare you boast honour and be so ignoble?
Did not you warrant me, upon that pawn

Which can take up no money, your blank honour,
That you would cure his jealousy, which affects him
Like a sharp sore, if I to ripen it
Would set that counterfeit face of scorn upon him
Only in show of disobedience – which   100
You won me to upon your protestation
To render me unstain'd to his opinion
And quit me of his jealousy forever?

Letoy   No, not unstain'd, by your leave, if you call
Unchastity a stain. But for his yellows,
Let me but lie with you and let him know it,
His jealousy is gone, all doubts are clear'd
And for his love and good opinion
He shall not dare deny it. Come, be wise,
And this is all; all is as good as done   110
To him already. Let't be so with us;
And trust to me, my power and your own
To make all good with him. If not – now mark –
To be reveng'd for my lost hopes (which yet
I prithee save), I'll put thee in his hands
Now, in his heat of fury, and not spare
To boast thou art my prostitute and thrust ye
Out of my gates to try't out by yourselves.

Diana   This you may do and yet be still a lord;
This can I bear and still be the same woman!   120
I am not troubled now. Your wooing oratory,
Your violent hands (made stronger by your lust),
Your tempting gifts and larger promises
Of honour and advancements were all frivolous;
But this last way of threats ridiculous
To a safe mind that bears no guilty grudge.
My peace dwells here, while yonder sits my judge:
And in that faith I'll die.

Enter JOYLESS *and* BYPLAY

Letoy	[*aside*] She is invincible! –
	Come, I'll relate you to your husband.
Joyless	No,
	I'll meet her with more joy than I receiv'd 130
	Upon our marriage day. My better soul,
	Let me again embrace thee.
Byplay	Take your dudgeon, sir.
	I ha' done you simple service.
Joyless	Oh, my lord,
	My lord, you have cur'd my jealousy. I thank you –
	And more your man – for the discovery;
	But most the constant means, my virtuous wife,
	Your medicine, my sweet lord.
Letoy	She has ta'en all
	I mean to give her, sir. [*To* BYPLAY] Now, sirrah, speak.
Byplay	I brought you to the stand from whence you saw
	How the game went.
Joyless	Oh, my dear, dear Diana. 140
Byplay	I seem'd to do it against my will, by which I gain'd
	Your bribe of twenty pieces.
Joyless	Much good do thee.
Byplay	But I assure you my lord give me order
	To place you there after it seems he had
	Well put her to't within.
Joyless	Stay, stay, stay, stay!
	Why may not this be then a counterfeit action,
	Or a false mist to blind me with more error?
	The ill I fear'd may have been done before,
	And all this but deceit to daub it o'er.
Diana	Do you fall back again?

Joyless	[*reaches for dagger*] Shugh, give me leave – 150
Byplay	I must take charge, I see, o'th' dagger again. [*Takes* JOYLESS's *dagger*]
Letoy	Come, Joyless, I have pity on thee. Hear me. I swear upon mine honour she is chaste.
Joyless	Honour! An oath of glass!
Letoy	I prithee, hear me. I tried and tempted her for mine own ends More than for thine.
Joyless	That's easily believ'd.
Letoy	And had she yielded, I not only had Rejected her – for it was ne'er my purpose, Heaven I call thee to witness, to commit A sin with her – but laid a punishment 160 Upon her greater than thou couldst inflict.
Joyless	But how can this appear?
Letoy	Do you know your father, lady?
Diana	I hope I am so wise a child.
Letoy	[*to* BYPLAY] Go call In my friend Truelock.
Byplay	[*to* JOYLESS] Take your dagger, sir; Now I dare trust you.
Letoy	Sirrah, dare you fool When I am serious? Send in Master Truelock. *Exit* BYPLAY
Diana	That is my father's name.
Joyless	Can he be here?
Letoy	Sir, I am neither conjurer nor witch,

	But a great fortune-teller that you'll find	
	You are happy in a wife, sir, happier – yes,	170
	Happier by a hundred thousand pound	
	Than you were yesterday.	

Joyless   [*to* DIANA]   So, so, now he's mad.

Letoy   I mean in possibilities: provided that
            You use her well and nevermore be jealous.

Joyless   Must it come that way?

Letoy   Look you this way, sir,
            When I speak to you. I'll cross your fortune else,
            As I am true Letoy.

Joyless   [*to* DIANA]   Mad, mad, he's mad.
            Would we were quickly out on's fingers yet.

Letoy   When saw you your wife's father? Answer me?

Joyless   He came for London four days before us.   180

Letoy   'Tis possible he's here then. Do you know him?

                        Enter TRUELOCK

Diana   Oh, I am happy in his sight. (*She kneels*) Dear sir.

Letoy   'Tis but so much knee-labour lost. Stand up,
            Stand up, and mind me.

Truelock   You are well met, son Joyless.

Joyless   How have you been conceal'd, and in this house?
            Here's mystery in this.

Truelock   My good lord's pleasure.

Letoy   Know, sir, that I sent for him and for you,
            Instructing your friend Blaze, my instrument,
            To draw you to my doctor with your son.
            Your wife, I knew, must follow. What my end   190

Was in't shall quickly be discover'd to you
In a few words of your supposed father.

Diana   Supposed father!

Letoy   Yes. Come, Master Truelock,
My constant friend of thirty years' acquaintance,
Freely declare with your best knowledge now
Whose child this is.

Truelock   Your honour does as freely
Release me of my vow, then, in the secret
I lock'd up in this breast these seventeen years
Since she was three days old?

Letoy   True, Master Truelock.
I do release you of your vow. Now speak.   200

Truelock   Now she is yours, my lord, your only daughter.
And know you, Master Joyless, for some reason
Known to my lord, and large reward to me,
She has been from the third day of her life
Reputed mine, and that so covertly,
That not her lady mother nor my wife
Knew to their deaths the change of my dead infant,
Nor this sweet lady. 'Tis most true we had
A trusty nurse's help, and secrecy
Well paid for, in the carriage of our plot.   210

Letoy   Now shall you know what mov'd me, sir. I was
A thing beyond a madman, like yourself
Jealous; and had that strong distrust and fancied
Such proofs unto myself against my wife
That I conceiv'd the child was not mine own
And scorn'd to father it. Yet I gave, to breed her
And marry her as the daughter of this gentleman,
Two thousand pound I guess you had with her.
But since your match, my wife upon her death-bed
So clear'd herself of all my foul suspicions –   220

Blest be her memory – that I then resolv'd
By some quaint way (for I am still Letoy)
To see and try her throughly; and so much
To make her mine as I should find her worthy.
And now thou art my daughter and mine heir,
Provided still (for I am still Letoy)
[*to* JOYLESS] You honourably love her and defy
The cuckold-making fiend, foul jealousy.

Joyless   My lord, 'tis not her birth and fortune, which
Do jointly claim a privilege to live   230
Above my reach of jealousy, shall restrain
That passion in me, but her well-tried virtue;
In the true faith of which I am confirm'd
And throughly cur'd.

Letoy   As I am true Letoy,
Well said. I hope thy son is cur'd by this too.

Enter BARBARA

Now Mistress Blaze! Here is a woman now!
I cur'd her husband's jealousy, and twenty more
I'th' town, by means I and my doctor wrought.

Barbara   Truly, my lord, my husband has ta'en bread
And drunk upon't that, under heaven, he thinks   240
You were the means to make me an honest woman,
Or, at the least, him a contented man.

Letoy   Ha' done, ha' done –

Barbara   Yes, I believe you have done!
And if your husband, lady, be cur'd, as he should be
And as all foolish jealous husbands ought to be,
I know what was done first if my lord took
That course with you as me –

Letoy   Prithee, what cam'st thou for?

Barbara	My lord, to tell you, as the doctor tells me, The bride and bridegroom both are coming on The sweetliest to their wits again.
Letoy	I told you.
Barbara	Now you are a happy man, sir, and I hope A quiet man.
Joyless	Full of content and joy.
Barbara	Content! So was my husband when he knew the worst He could by his wife. Now you'll live quiet, lady.
Letoy	Why flyest thou off thus, woman, from the subject Thou wert upon?
Barbara	I beg your honour's pardon. And now I'll tell you. Be it by skill or chance, Or both, was never such a cure as is Upon that couple! Now they strive which most Shall love the other.
Letoy	Are they up and ready?
Barbara	Up? Up and ready to lie down again; There is no ho with them! They have been in th'Antipodes to some purpose And now are risen and return'd themselves. He's her dear 'Per' and she is his sweet 'Mat'. His kingship and her queenship are forgotten, And all their melancholy and his travels pass'd And but suppos'd their dreams.
Letoy	'Tis excellent.
Barbara	Now, sir, the doctor – for he is become An utter stranger to your son, and so Are all about 'em – craves your presence And such as he's acquainted with.

250

260

270

Letoy	[*to* JOYLESS] Go, sir.
	And go you, daughter.
Barbara	[*aside*] Daughter! That's the true trick
	Of all old whoremasters, to call their wenches
	Daughters.
Letoy	Has he known you, friend Truelock, too?
Truelock	Yes, from his childhood.
Letoy	Go, then, and possess him,
	Now he is sensible, how things have gone,
	What art, what means, what friends have been employ'd
	In his rare cure; and win him, by degrees,
	To sense of where he is. Bring him to me; 280
	And I have yet an entertainment for him
	Of better settle-brain than drunkard's porridge
	To set him right. As I am true Letoy,
	I have one toy left. Go.
	Exeunt [TRUELOCK,] JOYLESS [*and* DIANA]
	And go you. Why stay'st thou?
Barbara	If I had been a gentlewoman born,
	I should have been your daughter too, my lord.
Letoy	But never as she is. You'll know anon.
Barbara	Neat city wife's flesh yet may be as good
	As your coarse country gentlewoman's blood. *Exit*
Letoy	Go with thy flesh to Turnbull shambles! – Ho, 290
	Within there!

Enter QUAILPIPE

Quailpipe	Here, my lord.
Letoy	The music, songs
	And dance I gave command for, are they ready?

Quailpipe	All, my good lord; and in good sooth I cannot
	Enough applaud your honour's quaint conceit
	In the design, so apt, so regular,
	So pregnant, so acute and so withal
	Poetice legitimate, as I
	May say justly with Plautus –

Letoy   Prithee, say no more,
But see upon my signal given they act
As well as I design'd.

Quailpipe   Nay, not so well,   300
My exact lord, but as they may, they shall.   *Exit*

Letoy   I know no flatterer in my house but this,
But for his custom I must bear with him.
'Sprecious, they come already. Now begin.

A solemn lesson upon the recorders. Enter TRUELOCK, JOYLESS,
and DIANA, PEREGRINE *and* MARTHA, DOCTOR
and BARBARA. LETOY *meets them.* TRUELOCK *presents*
PEREGRINE *and* MARTHA *to him. He salutes them. They seem*
to make some short discourse, then LETOY *appoints them to sit.*
PEREGRINE *seems something amazed. The music ceases*

Letoy   Again you are welcome, sir, and welcome all.

Peregrine   I am what you are pleas'd to make me, but
Withal so ignorant of mine own condition –
Whether I sleep, or wake, or talk, or dream;
Whether I be, or be not; or if I am,
Whether I do, or do not anything.   310
For I have had, if I now wake, such dreams,
And been so far transported in a long
And tedious voyage of sleep that I may fear
My manners can acquire no welcome where
Men understand themselves.

Letoy	This is music!
	Sir, you are welcome, and I give full power
	Unto your father and my daughter here, your mother,
	To make you welcome.

Peregrine   How! Your daughter, sir?

JOYLESS *whispers* PEREGRINE

Doctor   [*aside*] My lord, you'll put him back again if you
Trouble his brain with new discoveries.   320

Letoy   [*aside*] Fetch him you on again, then. Pray, are you
Letoy, or I?

Joyless   Indeed it is so, son.

Doctor   [*aside*] I fear your show will but perplex him too.

Letoy   [*aside*] I care not, sir. I'll have it to delay
Your cure awhile, that he recover soundly. –
Come, sit again; again you are most welcome.

A most untuneable flourish. Enter DISCORD
attended by Folly, Jealousy, Melancholy and Madness

There's an unwelcome guest, uncivil Discord,
That trains into my house her followers:
Folly and Jealousy, Melancholy and Madness.

Barbara   My husband presents Jealousy in the black   330
And yellow jaundied suit there, half like man
And t'other half like woman, with one horn
And ass-ear upon his head.

Letoy   [*aside*] Peace, woman.
[*To* PEREGRINE]   Mark what they do; but, by the way,
Conceive me this but show, sir, and device.

Peregrine   I think so.

Letoy   [*aside*]   How goes he back again now, doctor? Shugh!

Song in untuneable notes

Discord   Come forth my darlings, you that breed
           The common strifes that discord feed.
               Come in the first place, my dear Folly;
               Jealousy next; then Melancholy;   340
               And last come Madness, thou art he
               That bear'st th'effects of all those three.
           Lend me your aids, so Discord shall you crown
           And make this place a kingdom of our own.

*They dance. After a while they are broke off by a flourish
and the approach of HARMONY, followed by Mercury, Cupid,
Bacchus and Apollo. DISCORD and her faction fall down*

Letoy   See, Harmony approaches, leading on
           'Gainst Discord's factions four great deities:
           Mercury, Cupid, Bacchus and Apollo.
           Wit against Folly, Love against Jealousy,
           Wine against Melancholy and 'gainst Madness, Health.
           Observe the matter and the method.

Peregrine   Yes.   350

Letoy   And how upon the approach of Harmony
           Discord and her disorders are confounded.

Song

Harmony   Come Wit, come Love, come Wine, come Health,
           Maintainers of my commonwealth,
               'Tis you make Harmony complete,
               And from the spheres, her proper seat,
               You give her power to reign on earth
               Where Discord claims a right by birth.
           Then let us revel it while we are here
           And keep possession of this hemisphere.   360

*After a strain or two DISCORD cheers up her faction. They all
rise and mingle in the dance with HARMONY and the rest. Dance*

Letoy	Note there how Discord cheers up her disorders
	To mingle in defiance with the virtues.
	But soon they vanish,

Exeunt DISCORD [*and her followers*]

and the mansion quit
Unto the gods of health, love, wine and wit
Who triumph in their habitation new,
Which they have taken and assign to you;
In which they now salute you,

[HARMONY *and her followers*] *salute* [*and*] *exeunt*

bids you be
Of cheer and for it lays the charge on me.
And unto me you're welcome, welcome all.
Meat, wine and mirth shall flow, and what I see   370
Yet wanting in your cure supplied shall be.

Peregrine	Indeed, I find me well.
Martha	And so shall I
	After a few such nights more.
Barbara	Are you there?
	[*To* DIANA] Good madam, pardon errors of my tongue.
Diana	I am too happy made to think of wrong.
Letoy	We will want nothing for you that may please,
	Though we dive for it to th'Antipodes.

THE EPILOGUE

Doctor	Whether my cure be perfect yet or no
	It lies not in my doctorship to know.
	Your approbation may more raise the man 380
	Than all the College of Physicians can,
	And more health from your fair hands may be won
	Than by the strokings of the seventh son.

Peregrine   And from our travels in th'Antipodes
                     We are not yet arriv'd from off the seas;
                     But on the waves of desp'rate fears we roam
                     Until your gentler hands do waft us home.

                                                         [*Exeunt omnes*]

FINIS

[THE AUTHOR TO THE READER]

Courteous Reader,

You shall find in this book more than was presented upon the stage, and left out of the presentation for superfluous length (as some of the players pretended). I thought good all should be inserted according to the allowed original, and as it was at first intended for the Cockpit stage, in the right of my most deserving friend Mr William Beeston, unto whom it properly appertained. And so I leave it to thy perusal as it was generally applauded and well acted at Salisbury Court.

                              Farewell,

                                                      Ri. Brome

GLOSSARIAL NOTES

Dedicatory Epistle

3   *William, Earl of Hertford*   William Seymour (1588–1660), second Earl of Hertford, became a Privy Councillor and Marquis of Hertford in 1640

To censuring Critics

1   *Jonson's alive*   Ben Jonson, Brome's mentor and one-time master, died on 6 August 1637

3   *Apollo's pensioners*   poets (Apollo is the god of poetry)

4   *abortive elegies*   unnecessary (if Jonson is imagined still to be alive). A collection of elegies on Jonson was published in 1638.

5   *Taylor*   John Taylor, a waterman, was a prolific and popular writer of the early seventeenth century, nicknamed 'The Water Poet'.
    goose quill   pen (geese were also associated with folly)

8   *Elysian coast*   from the Elysian fields, heaven in classical mythology

10   *stole*   stolen
    grove of bays   associated with Apollo. Poets were crowned with wreaths of bay (hence poet laureate)

18   *old toys*   stale light or facetious compositions

20   *Volpone, Sejanus, Catiline*   three plays by Ben Jonson

23   *C.G.*   probably Charles Gerbier, writer and associate of Brome

To the Author

2   *Methought*   it seemed to me
    Antipodes   literally 'those who dwell directly opposite to each other on the globe, so that the soles of their feet are as it were planted against each other, especially those who occupy this position in regard to us' (*OED*, *sb.* 1), hence 'places on the surfaces of the earth directly opposite each other'

5   *scull mistook*   my boat landed at the wrong place; also (depending on *skull*, brain, mind) I was mistaken

6   *strand*   shore

10   *Pierian maid*   muse; Pieria in North Thessaly was reputed home of the nine Muses.

11   *prate*   chatter
     it boots not   it doesn't matter
13   *priv'lege*   advantage, right
     that crew   those idiots
15   *Rob. Chamberlain*   minor poet and playwright of the mid seventeenth
     century

Dramatis Personae

2   *BLAZE*   from the verb to blaze, to emblazon, to describe heraldically
     herald painter   painter of coats of arms
4   *Hughball*   from ball, a large pill
7   *LETOY*   *toy*, amorous sport, amusement or entertainment, whim or
     caprice – all associated with Letoy
     fantastic   whimsical, capricious, extravagant, eccentric
8   *QUAILPIPE*   pipe or whistle used to lure quails – suggests therefore a
     high-pitched nasal voice, often used to characterise curates. Cf. Roger
     L'Estrange, *State Divinity* 14 (1661) 'To give over their Quailpiping in a
     pulpit to catch silly women'; Dekker (1603), *Wonderful Year*, F3^V, 'the
     Justice…held his nose hard betweene his fore-finger and his thumbe,
     and speaking in that wise … cryed out in that quaile-pipe voice, that if
     they were Londoners, away with them to Limbo' (cited in *OED*).
11   *BYPLAY*   action carried on aside while the main action proceeds; an
     appropriate name for the improvising actor in the play within a play
     conceited   witty

Prologue

1   *Opinion*   fashion
2   *daintiness*   fastidiousness
     of late   recently
3   *possess'd*   captivated
     a sort   certain people
9   *sportive*   playful
12   *late sublimed*   recently exalted (i.e. by death)
17   *trac'd*   travelled; written
18   *Phoebean light*   the light of poetic inspiration (Phoebus is another name
     for Apollo)
20   *weakest branch o'th' stage*   comedy

22   *slight*   trivial
      nigh   near
30   *admiration*   wonder

1.1

3   *want*   lack
4   *that time's calamity*   refers to the recent outbreak of plague
5   *high*   divine
6   *half-pin'd*   half starved
17   *advertis'd*   notified
23   *recipes*   prescriptions
27   *stupid*   stupefied, stunned
34   *for a dead horse*   for nothing (proverbial)
36   *wholesale day*   day on which everything was sold
51   *painting*   cosmetics, make-up
52   *philosopher's stone*   the goal of alchemy, believed to turn base metals into gold
61   *flockbed*   bed with a coarsely stuffed mattress (using wool or cotton waste)
62   *down*   a featherbed (i.e. of high quality and comfort)
65   *men of place*   officials
66   *understood not*   could not distinguish
67   *fell on praemunires*   ran into trouble (a praemunire is a writ against illegal practices)
68   *divers*   several
73   *In a pitch o'er the bar*   by being disbarred (punning on falling head first over a hurdle?)
74   *moons*   months
75   *Went*   was walking
77   *calling*   profession
79   *horn-mad*   mad with jealousy (horns are associated with cuckoldry)
83   *'Slid*   by God's eyelid, common oath
      he has almost catch'd me   he almost caught me out
84   *parties*   individuals
89   *'Sfoot*   by God's foot, common oath
92   *set out*   describe, advertise
      been a professor   in the profession
96   *goes*   behaves, dresses

101　*ail something*　have something wrong with them
103　*careful*　solicitous, sorrowful, anxious
108　*still*　always
111　*melancholy*　believed to result from excess of black bile
118　*crosses*　troubles, vexations
119　*late*　recent
123　*Divers*　a few
124　*travailing*　labouring
　　　Addicted　devoted
129　*distemper*　derangement, disease
130　*next*　quickest
140, 144, 145　*still*　always
142–3　*he made suit / To be made one in it*　he petitioned to join it
147　*extravagant*　wandering
148　*stay'd*　prevented
150　*abroad*　away from home
151　*undertake*　take on the case of
153, 166, 168　*undertake*　see 151n.; here with sexual innuendo
160　*utters*　demonstrates, shows
161　*several*　various, different
162　*Objects*　sights
163　*anon*　at once
165　*presently*　instantly
170　*yellow spots*　signs of jealousy
175　*travail*　labour
178　*tympany*　swelling (especially in reference to pregnancy)
178ff.　The wonders described in this and the following speeches appear in
　　　the *Travels* of Sir John Mandeville, a fourteenth-century traveller, which
　　　were written in 1364 and first published in 1496.
179　*Pygmies*　still thought, in the early seventeenth century, to be mythical
　　　or fabulous: Mandeville, chapter 64, 'Of the Land of Pigmie, the people
　　　whereof are but three spans long'
180　*Gryphons*　fabulous animals with the wings of an eagle and body and
　　　the hind quarters of a lion: Mandeville, chapter 85
182　*Christendom*　countries professing Christianity taken collectively;
　　　imagined by Barbara to be a distant foreign land
184　*Mount in Cornwall*　St Michael's Mount, near Penzance
186　*An*　if

188 *Cathaya*   China: Mandeville, chapters 66–75
189 *Great Khan*   Emperor of China: Mandeville, chapters 68, 76, 'The
     Emperour, the great Caane, hath three Wives, and the principall wife
     was Prester Iohn's Daughter'
     Prester John   mythic priest king of Ethiopa
190 *clown*   fool
191 *Unto the*   compared with
192 *Paradise*   identified with the site of the Garden of Eden in Mesopotamia
198 *warrant*   promise
209 *match*   marry
     wits   bodily faculties
218 *trow*   do you suppose
223–6, 247–50 These lines suggest that Letoy, not Blaze, may have fathered
     Barbara's children.
228 *fac'd me down and stood on't*   browbeat me and insisted on it
230 *Great Turk*   Turkish Emperor
233 *Train'd up to men*   brought up until they are men
240 *to making*   for making one
241 *past*   no longer
245 *fain*   gladly
250 *charge*   accuse
254 *wanton maid*   amorous, naughty girl
255 *clipp'd and clapp'd*   hugged and patted
259 *piece of innocence*   innocent, naïve girl
260 *use to*   normally
262 *use me as he should*   i.e. make love to me
267 *will say*   say
271 *use to*   habitually
275 *wage*   stake, wager
276 *ease*   cure

1.2

1   *arms and pedigree*   coat of arms and genealogical table
2   *herald's painter*   see note on Dramatis Personae
6   *Ex origine, ab antiquo*   from the ancient origins of my family
    fetch'd   traced
7   *descents*   generations

9   *Conqueror*   William, Duke of Normandy, invaded England in 1066 and made himself King William I.

17   *primo Ricardi Secundi*   the first year of the reign of Richard II (1377–8)

19   *Mark the end*   wait for it, let me finish

20   *my humour*   temperament, hence whim

23   *beholding*   indebted

26   *Battens*   feeds, fattens up
      cost   expense, i.e. interest on loans

31   *Abroad*   in public
      cloth o'baudkin   rich shot silk, originally woven with gold thread and silk
      broadcloth   plain woven black cloth

38   *shows*   display
      braveries   finery

39   *ring*   'A circlet of metal suspended from a post which each of a number of riders endeavoured to carry off on the point of his lance' (*OED, sb.* 1 4a)

41   *pitch the bar*   throw the bar (thick rod of iron or wood) as a trial of strength

42   *crack the cudgels*   fight with cudgels (short thick sticks)
      pate   head

45   *Polecats*   small predatory mammals; figuratively, prostitutes

46   *mad grigs*   wild lads
      base   children's team game whereby anyone caught outside his/her defined 'base' is taken prisoner

47   *breathe*   exercise briskly
      barley-break   old country game resembling running at base (tag), played by couples

52   *in substance*   essentially

57   *within myself*   in my own home or at my expense

59   *of quality*   professionally expert

62   *bravery*   finery

63   *undoes*   ruins

64   *there's my bravery*   that's what I boast of; literally 'There are my fine clothes'

64 SD   *Hautboys*   loud double-reed woodwind instruments from which the oboe later developed

68   *to boot*   also, into the bargain

69   *Caesar*   probably Nero, a lover of theatrical spectacle
      English earl   probably the Earl of Leicester, patron of the first company of London actors in the 1570s

71   *outvied*   excelled, outdone
73   *quality*   occupation
78–9   *And make … too*   a jesting reference to the vogue for plays by aristocratic or titled poets in the late 1630s
80   *horse-tricks*   tricks by performing horses (such as the famous Morocco, 'the dancing horse', exhibited by his master, Banks)
82   *May-games, play-games*   merry-makings, foolish sports, frolics
84   *brave*   fine, splendid
85   *stays prepar'd*   is ready
86   *ready with your grace*   ready to say grace (Quailpipe is Letoy's chaplain)
87   *meat*   food
     rambled   wandered
91, 92   *wants*   lacks

1.3

8   *angle*   corner
     nether   under
10   *warrant*   guarantee
11–12   *Galen, Hippocrates, Avicen, Dioscorides*   ancient Greek and Arab medical authorities
14   *chamber*   room
19   *Bewray*   betray, expose, reveal
     intimation   hint
28   *Drake*   Sir Francis Drake, first English circumnavigator of the world
29   *didapper*   dabchick (small water bird)
30   *Ca'ndish*   Thomas Cavendish, the second English circumnavigator (1586–8)
     Hawkins   Sir John, or his son Sir Richard, both famous travellers
     Frobisher   Martin Frobisher attempted to find the North West route round North America to China.
33–45   *the trees … year*   this information comes from Mandeville, chapter 91
40   *Stay*   stop
     else   if you don't believe me
41   *No … seen't*   It's as true as if I'd seen it
52   'That cure would be worth a fee of half my land.'
54   *encumbrances*   literally, liabilities, hence Joyless's jealousy
63   *garb*   manner, behaviour, fashion
71   *Paphos Isle*   Paphos, a city on the island of Cyprus, sacred to Venus

77–8   *beggingly ... returns*   have pleaded to invest in trading ventures

80   *milliner*   vendor of fancy wares and articles of apparel, especially hats

82   *unprotected*   without a guard to protect him against arrest by his creditors

83   *old Exchange*   Sir Thomas Gresham's Royal Exchange, a business centre
        located between Cornhill and Threadneedle Street in the city of
        London

84   *pitch*   pick, choose

85–6   *foot to foot / Against*   the literal sense of the Greek words *anti-* (against),
        podes (feet)

98–100 *without ... breasts*   cf. *Othello* and *The Tempest*

106   *supposite*   placed directly below (*OED* cites this as only occurrence in
        this sense)

109   *manners*   morals

118   *There's precious bribing then!*   That must cost a great deal in bribes.

121   *I ...else*   I really wish they could

126   *art*   skill

127   *o'ersway*   govern, rule

128   *art's above nature*   reversal of usual assertion that nature is superior to art

130   *quality*   rank

134   *I warrant you*   I'll bet

135   *charge*   command, order

136   *tender*   care for, value

140   *trim*   neat

142   *gossips*   godparents'

144   *tittle-tattle*   trivial, chattering

149   *tercel*   male hawk
        lanneret   male lanner (falcon)

155   *train-scents*   exercise of hounds by dragging something strongly-
        smelling along the ground to create a scent for them to follow

165   *At ring*   see 1.2.39n.; here with likely sexual innuendo

166   *painted*   made up

167   *servants*   lovers

180   *As*   as if

185   *handicrafts*   artisans

188   *divines*   ministers of religion

189   *wranglers*   disputers

195   *hirelings*   hired servants
        clowns   rustics, country people

198 *Precisest* most puritanical
208 *hear* listen to
210 *auspicate* give a fortunate start to, wish well to
216 *wants* lacks
217 *stay'd* delayed
219 *weigh anchor* raise the anchor
220 *only stay* are waiting only
229 *save* pick up, retrieve; look after, take care of
230 *In sooth* truly

2.1

2 *takes* succeeds
4 *fancy* contrivance, i.e. the play
5 *cried up* praised as
  fancy invention
8 *fancies* whims
9 *still* forever
12 *After* at the speed of
13 *shall awake anon* is due to wake soon
15, 16 *perfect* word perfect
17 *makes such shifts extempore* improvises so well
20 *poetic furies* inspired poets (from *furor poeticus* – poetic frenzy)
23 *fribble* stagger through, improvise
24 *mimic fellow* actor
25 *entertain'd* employed
27 *must* will have to
31 *put him to't* don't spare him (with probable sexual innuendo)
33 *Hast wrought* have you persuaded
34 *suffer* permit
36 *in's* in his
37 *spur his jealousy off o'the legs* make him collapse with jealousy
40 *and's* and his
48 *targets* shields
49 *what a rude coil* what a racket
54 *that name* i. e. knave
55 *ready* dressed
56 *shape* stage dress, costume

58, 60   *want*   lack

60   *beaver*   shoes made of beaver fur – normal material for hats, therefore
an Antipodean reversal
leather cap   cap made of shoe leather

64   *Certes*   certainly

66   *capital*   suitable for the head

69–90   In this and the following speeches Brome rewrites and versifies
Hamlet's advice to the players, *Hamlet* 3.2.1–45

71   *seesaw sack-a-down*   onomatapoeic nonsense – seems to refer to the old
nursery rhyme, 'See-saw, sacradown; / Which is the way to London
town? / One foot up and the other foot down, / That is the way to
London town', I. & P. Opie, *Oxford Dictionary of Nursery Rhymes* (1951).
University actors are satirised for never speaking and walking at the
same time in *The Return from Parnassus*, 4.3, where Kempe thus describes
them: 'The slaves are somewhat proud, and, besides, it is good sport, in
a part, to see them never speake in their walke, but at the end of the
stage, just as though in walking with a fellow we should never speake
but at a stile, a gate, or a ditch, when a man can go no further' (Baker).

72   *Hercules Furens*   leading character in Seneca's tragedy of the same name,
hence ranting actor

73, 98   *audients'*   listeners, hearers (*OED* B *sb.*)

76   *fibulating*   fiddling

77   *band-strings*   laces to fasten a clerical collar

81   *singles, doubles*   dance steps

82   *dancing masters*   teachers of dancing bears
Bear-garden   bear-baiting arena in Southwark on the south bank of the
Thames; by this date the bear-garden had been rebuilt as the Hope
playhouse, where bear-baiting still took place

85   *feat*   trick, turn

86   *They gather wind by firking up their breeches*   they hitch up their trousers to
give them time to recover their breath

90   *if*   provided that they are

94   *fancy*   imaginings

98   *interlocutions*   conversations

100   *elder*   older

101   *Tarleton*   Richard Tarleton, died 1588: in his time famous for comic
improvisation.
Kemp   Will Kemp, died about 1603–4. Another leading comedian

thought to have improvised (though there is less clear evidence than in the case of Tarleton).

104 *spent their wits*   exhausted, expended their comic inventiveness
110 *gave me light*   informed me (playing on Blaze's name)
116 *sunk past rising*   irrevocably ruined (perhaps as a result of the recent plague, see 1.1.4, 'that time's calamity')
119 *a person*   an actor
131 *toy*   entertainment
133 *toys*   literally children's toys
135 *Time was*   there was a time when
138 *wanting*   missing
139 *study*   learn
169 *from*   contrary to
171 *post*   hurry
175 *plain*   simply dressed
176 *brave*   finely dressed

2.2

0.1 *sea gowns*   tough water-resistant garments for sailors or passengers at sea
2   *Determines*   is coming to an end
11   *phantasms*   fantasies
14   *somniferous*   drowsy, soporific
15   *calenture*   fever or sun stroke (caused by tropical heat)
20   *seven Christian champions*   The heroes of Richard Johnson's popular romance *The Seven Champions of Christendom* (1596) are the patron saints of England, Scotland, Wales, Ireland, France, Italy and Spain.
21   *David*   patron saint of Wales, spends seven years in a magical sleep
     leek bed   Brome's comic addition (the leek being the emblem of Wales)
24   *presently*   immediately
26   *upper world*   northern hemisphere
27   *them*   inhabitants of the northern hemisphere
33   *clime*   region
34–5 *Of equal . . . London*   whose climate is the same as that of London
37   *I never was at London*   evidence of the extent of Peregrine's obsession
     Cry you mercy   forgive me
44   *weeds*   clothes
49   *Our far-fetch'd title*   the title of the main play, *The Antipodes*, is used also for the play within the play

53	*Because* in order that

55–9	'It is almost impossible to say anything without someone claiming that it is a personal attack on him, especially if it is vicious or absurd enough'

60	*prejudice* personal attack or injury

61	*satiric timist* topical satirist

62	*tax* reprove

touch at   point to

65	*degree* social rank

from kaiser to the clown   from king to countryman

67–8	*if … syllables* if you had not drawled out your speech so drowsily

70	*reader* cleric in minor orders or lay person who reads the lessons in church

71	*Out of his function* when he's not working

76–7	*Children / Of his Black Revels* ' pun: (1) Children of the Revels; (2) their theatre, Blackfriars. Brome wrote for the Children of the King's Revels during the first year or so of his contract with Salisbury Court' (Haaker)

78	*fain* gladly

82	*anon* at once

82 SD	*Flourish* fanfare

83	*Why … office* why don't you arrest me

86–8	*A … it* reverses the common joke that being arrested gives you an ache in your shoulder (sergeants arrested by laying a hand on the shoulder of suspects)

91	*charter of the city* the city's laws

92	*forfeited* ignored, forgotten

varlets   low-born rascals, knaves

94	*catchpolls* arresting officers

95	*would / Have been* wished to be

97	*fetch breath* get my breath back

100	*puppy* term of contempt (implies that Byplay is young)

104	*was not touch'd* have not been arrested

104–5	*made / An end by composition* reached an agreement

111	*mend* increase

118	*squire* attendant, inferior

119	*covert-barne* The condition normally of an English married woman under the subjection of her husband – here applied to the husband.

trespass   offence

126	*humour* attitude, sentiment, disposition

127 *mercer*   trader in fabrics

130 *lays*   lies in wait, arranges, plans

135 *portion*   dowry, another Antipodean reversal; in England wives brought dowries to their husbands

137, 140 *jointure*   marriage settlement; in the Antipodes the estate settled on the husband by the wife

146 *Good, still*   'be quiet, my good fellow.'

147 *woman*   servant

148 *half these words*   with half this trouble

151 *handmaid*   servant

160 *Precious*   by God's precious , a common oath from 'by Christ's precious blood' (also ''Sprecious' at 5.2.304)

164, 165 *charge*   task

166 *wild*   unruly

171 *stay*   support

177 *In sooth*   truly

179–80 *How …today*   how efficient you were in seeing your father went to school today

183 *Domine, domine duster*   'master, master duster'; *duster*, presumably for cleaning a blackboard, hence dusty with chalk, 'dry-as-dust'

191 *bain't*   illiterate form of *be not*, are not

193 *pay*   punish

194 *gallows-clappers*   good-for-nothings; from the swinging of the body to and fro from the gallows like the clapper of a bell

197, 217 *strangers*   foreigners

198 *speaks extempore*   is improvising

199 *dogged*   cruel

200 *Fie upon him*   exclamation of disgust or reproach

201 *fair*   advanced

204–5 *wip'd / My lips*   'got the better of me', 'that's one in the eye for me'

214 *speechless*   incapable of speech

210 *These*   the three old men

223 *Gratias*   thanks

225 *the while*   in the meantime

228 *proper*   handsome

248 *comedians*   actors (in general)

249 *Shall pause the while*   will have an interval meanwhile: a regular practice of the indoor playhouses of the early seventeenth century

250 *must not*   don't have to
     here   in the Antipodes; in Letoy's house; in London
253 *confines*   regions, territories
258 *viands, beverage*   food and drink
260 *Thou tak'st him right*   that's a good suggestion

3.1

5   *catastrophe*   dénouement
8   *tie*   compel
20 *firk*   drive, urge
22 *octavus Michaelis*   7 October – eight days after Michaelmas Day, one of
     the days appointed for returning legal writs
25 *Goes ... brave*   are lawyers so tattered and poets so finely dressed
28 *bill of parcels*   itemised account
36, 44 *Imprimis*   first
37 *character*   handwriting
     orthography   spelling
40 *Better than ours do custards*   An enormous bowl of custard, into which a
     jester jumped fully clothed, figured prominently at the Lord Mayor's
     annual banquet.
42, 43 *want*   lack
46 *holy vestals of Bridewell*   ironic because Bridewell was a prison (which
     would have prostitutes among its inmates), though in anti-London it
     would presumably be a church
48 *groats*   silver coins worth fourpence
50 *sessions*   sessions of the court
     shrievalty   period of office as sheriff
51 *Newgate*   most notorious of the London prisons, so presumably a
     famous church in anti-London
56 *precise*   puritanical
57 *sober sisterhood*   puritan women
61 *distich*   poetic couplet
     graven   engraved
     thumb-ring   ring formerly worn on the thumb, often with a seal
63 *alder predecessors*   predecessors as aldermen
     brethren   colleagues
64 *curious piece*   ingenious composition

65   *pieces*   gold coins
69   *common councilman*   member of the city's governing body
     shrieve   sheriff
71   *Here's a sum towards indeed*   'he's going to get a large sum for that',
     'that's going to earn him a lot'
77   *priz'd*   valued
     crooked deformed; Diana possibly takes it in its other meaning –
     unchaste
82   *aldermanikin*   little or young alderman (only recorded instance in *OED*)
84   *Katherine Stubbes*   wife of Philip Stubbes, for whom he wrote *A Crystal
     glass for Christian women* (1591). She was offered as an example of
     Christian virtue and died at the age of eighteen in childbirth.
88   *peccavi*   I have sinned
89   *bigness*   importance, authority
90   *Jamque ... ignis*   Ovid's *Metamorphoses*, XV, 871–2, translated by George
     Sandys (1638) as 'And now the worke is ended, which, *Iove*'s rage / Nor
     fire, [nor Sword shall raze, nor eating Age]' (XV, 983–5, the words in
     square brackets are not in Brome's quotation)
100 *posy*   short motto
108 *composition*   settlement out of court
110–11 *compound / A difference*   succeed in arbitration
111–12 *toss ... judgement*   'won't take the risk of an unpredictable verdict'
111 *toss nor bandy*   knock back and forth – tennis metaphor
112 *Into the hazard*   continuing the tennis image, 'hazard' referred to each of
     the winning openings of a tennis court
113 *no marvel*   it's no surprise
114 *occasion*   opportunity
117 *battery*   assault
120 *By this fair hilt*   I swear on my sword
121 *stitch'd my sides*   made my sides ache
123 *I put it up*   endure it, put up with it (literally, 'sheathe my sword')
124 *It is up*   literally, your sword is sheathed again, i.e. it's already resolved
126 *feathermaker*   supplier of feathers for wearing in a hat
132, 137, 156   *duns, dunned*   pesters, pestered
134 *he ... breaks my sleeps*   wakes me up (either in dreams, which 'haunts'
     suggests, or by literally disturbing him)
135 *this*   the feather in his hat
142 *Compound*   resolve, settle

146 *marks*   a mark was worth two thirds of a pound, or 13 shillings and 4 pence

148 *So*   if, provided that

158 *still*   always

160 SD   *Buff woman*   woman in a buff coat, stout coat of buff leather (often worn by soldiers)

162 *militasters*   weekend soldiers without military skill or knowledge
calfskin   calf suggests fool – therefore pejorative

163 *trow*   do you think

164 *tavern garrison*   the habitual drinkers in a tavern

168 *makes … him*   beats him; takes revenge by infidelity to him (or perhaps gets on top of him in sexual sense?)

171 *constr'ing and piercing of your scribblings*   deciphering and scrutinising your papers

172 *Cry mercy*   excuse me

174 *marshal's court*   a court overseen by the steward of the King's household, with jurisdiction over domestic matters

176, 178 *passages*   progress. In line 178 the woman interprets it as meaning entrails.

178 *cause*   case

179 *windy workings*   breaking wind

179–80 *fizzlings at / The bar*   discreet farting in court

190 *shrewd*   hurtful

198 *retribution*   reward

202–3 *when … occasions*   when my present resources are not equal to my own needs

203–4 *oppress … breath*   importune me with fruitless requests

206 *ragged*   beggarly, tattered

208 *Absolute*   perfect

211 *instant want*   urgent need

219 *crown*   silver coin worth five shillings

224 *souse*   various parts of a pig pickled for eating
pot-butter   butter potted or salted for preservation

225 *chamber*   apartment

227 *lay upon my back*   spend on clothes

233 *Jack-a-Lent*   a figure to be pelted during Lent – presumably in a bright coloured suit (to help his eyesight, by his aiming at the figure as a target)

234 *sarcenet*   taffeta

235 *one*   i.e. a suit
236 *politic*   cunning
238 *If he exact not that*   if he doesn't enforce payment of it
243 *be …'em*   Actors owned shares in their companies.
     be put in for   be proposed as a sharer (becomes sexual in Joyless's response)
253 SD *Fortune my foe*   the so-called 'hanging tune', sung by condemned men: 'Fortune, my foe, why dost thou frown on me? / And will thy favours never greater be? / Wilt thou, I say, forever breed me pain, / And wilt thou not restore my joys again?' (text from F. Beaumont, *The Knight of the Burning Pestle*, 5.239)
260 *Keep fast*   hang on to
     forgo your wit   be foolish
270 *How*   why
272 *stop their mouths*   silence them
274 *In forma pauperis*   in the form of paupers; i.e. without paying a fee
277 *get aforehand so for law*   accumulate the money needed for legal fees
281 *Till … Jews*   viz., to Christianity, i.e. never
288 *tiring-house*   backstage area used as a dressing room and to store props
289 *properties*   stage props
292 *bugbears*   hobgoblins, objects of terror
294 *pasteboard marchpanes*   cardboard cakes of almond and sugar (marzipan)
298 *monuments*   effigies
299 *uncouth and of various aspects*   strange and diverse appearance
300 *dive not to his thoughts*   I can't guess what he was thinking
302 *force*   strength
303 *puissant*   mighty
304 *Bevis*   Bevis of Hampton, dragon-slaying hero of a popular romance
307 *Cyclops*   one-eyed monster in Homer's *Odyssey*
308 *jiggumbobs*   knick-knacks, toys
314 *mammocks*   shreds, bits and pieces
319 *sooth'd*   humoured
321 *reduce*   adapt
325 *event*   outcome
327 *state*   pomp, ceremony
330 *absolute action*   consummate, perfect performance
332 *move*   persuade
336–7 *the name / Of sober chastity*   Diana was patroness of virginity

338   *beast*   a horned beast; a cuckold

340–1   *Your ...country*   you were too jealous to leave me behind in the country

346   *hazard*   risk

357   *housewif'ry*   economy, thriftiness

362   *free*   a member of a company or guild
pointmakers   points were tagged laces or cords to attach hose to doublet. Byplay is punning on 'legal point'.

371–2   *shake ... any*   get lost. Loss of ears was a usual criminal sentence.

373   *Preserve ... summers*   save their breath to guess at the coming weather; a trivial activity the lawyers could be better employed in.

379   *grace*   thank, show favour to

389   *Do you double with me*   are you complaining again

398   *empt*   empty

401   *flinching*   reluctant

404   *is terrible*   inspires fear or awe

408   *shopbook*   account book

416   *place of worship*   prominent place or rank

422   *fall*   abandon
draw   withdraw

423   *alack-a-day*   woe on the day, alas

430   *drive a half-trade*   share our trade

431   *Break with*   break their promise to, break off their affair with

432   *broken*   bankrupt

439   *consume*   squander

445, 446   *stand out*   resist (with sexual innuendo in following line)

453   *from the point*   irrelevant

467–8   *use/ Urbanity*   be courteous

469   *by calling*   by occupation, business

478   *feeling*   desire (both for money and sex)

490   *warrant*   guarantee

491   *e'en*   just

500   *Vouchsafe*   condescend

501   *freedom*   membership in a city company

502   *our purse*   the company's resources

511   *warrant*   promise

512   *cozen'd*   cheated

516   *property*   stage prop

517 *lath*   stage swords were made of lath (thin narrow strips of wood)
521 *trusty*   trustworthy
523 *banquet*   light refreshment

4.1

3   *passages*   what's going on
7   *close*   secret, concealed
9   *single*   one at a time
     game bear   bear that is being baited
12   *courses*   bouts, attacks, rounds
     great   large
17   *bills*   flyers, advertisements: often handwritten
20   *meditations*   book of religious doctrines or sermons
21   *royal game*   pastime favoured by the King
29   *one side venison*   according to Jonson the left-side, where the heart lies
     (based on implicit pun on *hart/heart*, see Jonson, *Magnetic Lady*,
     Induction)
30   *good author*   possibly Jonson
31   *baubles*   toys, playthings
33–4 *in due / Season*   in due course
41   *obscure*   cover
43   *Publish*   show off, display
45   *ass*   servingman speaks of himself as a beast of burden
48   *this book*   himself and the clothes he is wearing
51   *dainty*   pretty
54   *mowing*   reaping (*mowe* also meant 'copulate' in Scots dialect)
55   *may …company*   will you be good enough to keep me company
60   *a copy of your countenance*   pretence, hypocrisy
62   *known*   i.e. carnally
63   *half a piece*   half a gold piece
63–4 *deceiv'd … nose*   'you couldn't be more deceived' (possible suggestions
     of 'nose' would include syphilis, as the nose was the most visible part to
     be affected)
73   *turn*   purpose (sexual)
75   *Gip … fagh*   Get lost, old man!
79   *jade*   worthless horse, hack; hence 'slut'
87   *Hear me*   let me tell you, hear from me
89   *precepts*   orders

102 *Counter* debtors' prison

105 *at large* free

119 SD *prize* contest, fencing match

127 *harlots* rogues, beggars (male as well as female)

134 *pass'd on me* sentenced me

148 *as* as if

153 *spend* exhaust

161 *proper* specific, peculiar, fitting (oblique allusion to phrase from Lily's Latin Grammar *'propria quae maribus'* = those things which are proper to males)

162 *takes a taste of sense* is beginning to show sense

163 *reduce* adapt

164 *These* women and man-scold

165 *qualified* regulated

170 *My ... onions* my tavern meal of pumpkins baked with onions

171 *clowns* rustics

musk melons oriental melons (expensive because imported)

172 *ninepins* game like skittles or bowling

173 *tokens* small change made of base metal

pigeon-holes game 'like our modern *bagatelle*, where there was a machine with arches for the balls to run through, resembling the cavities made for pigeons in a dove-house', Halliwell, *Dictionary of Archaisms and Provincialisms* (1889)

174 *'Snails* by God's nails (referring to Christ nailed on the cross), common oath

Is my poke bottom broke Is there a hole in my pocket?

175 *A pox o'ertake thee now* may you catch the pox (pox was a venereal disease) – common expletive

176 *breech* backside

177 *In earnest?* Do you mean it?

179 *hold* grip

180 *currying* grooming

182 *afore* '"before you came along" – but punning on "in front". Sodomy, like women on top [1.3.141] is an antipodean sexual act' (Parr)

189 *twice and once* 'If I've told you once, I've told you a thousand times' or 'once and for all'

191 *of a* since I was

193 *nock'd i'th' fashion* slung fashionably behind me

194 *back-guard*   to protect my back, or backside

196 *I had as lief*   I'd as soon

199 *dainty*   fine, good

202 *burn daylight*   are wasting time

   the ale may sour   i.e. before we reach the pub (an old joke)

203 *rude silken clowns*   crude countrymen dressed in silk

204 *watermen*   Thames boatmen

   carmen   carters, who transport both goods and passengers

205 *conditions*   occupations

212 *care*   solicitude

212–219 *Still … service*   carman uses effusive court rhetoric

216 *were else*   would otherwise be

219 *devoir*   duty

226–7 *draw … gallows*   among the carmen's duties was transporting the
   condemned to execution

227.1 *Sedan-man*   Sedan chairs were introduced into London in the 1630s
   and faced strong opposition from carmen and watermen whose trade
   they threatened.

229 *just*   true

232 *withal*   with

233 *golden number*   connected with the Golden Age, characterised by
   prosperity and happiness; presumably with joking reference to the
   tavern sign of two fools' heads with the caption 'we three logger-heads
   be', implying that a third fool is looking at the sign, cf. *Twelfth Night*
   2.3.16–17. In Pythagorean philosophy, three is the perfect number,
   composed of all that comes before it.

234 *next of best*   nearest good tavern

238 *Importing*   signifying

238–9 *occurrences / And passages*   events and news

241 *advertisements*   news

241–2 *both / Our universities*   Oxford and Cambridge were then the only
   universities in England.

245 *this progress*   during the King's last journey round the country

248–50 *We … dispatches*   Taverns were places where news circulated, and
   Londoners often sent newsletters of notable events to correspondents in
   the country.

248 *gallant*   fine fellow (ironic)

256 *In sooth*   indeed

261 *they ...notes*   they must change their tunes
262 *Or ... coats*   to dress them according to their behaviour (reminder of
     the sumptuary laws dictating the clothing materials permitted for wear
     by each class or rank)
265 *New England*   North American colonies. In lines 265-6 Hughball
     applauds Peregrine for seeing them as a source for good advice about
     government.
266 *The ... none*   perhaps because there had been no parliament since
     Charles I dissolved it in 1629
270–1 *puritan ... lie*   Antipodean reversal of truth-telling puritan tradesmen
     and proverbially mendacious travellers
274 *natural fool*   born half-wit
275 *schismatic*   heretic
276 *scrivener*   professional copyist (cf. 3.368–9 n. about loss of ears)
277 *parish clerk*   minor cleric, curate
279 *Bellarmine*   Catholic controversialist against Protestantism
281 *Beyond the line*   past the Equator
282 *studious for a*   sensitive to the needs of
283 *projectors*   promoters or speculators
288 *jacks*   machines to turn spits for roasting meat, which were previously
     turned by children
295 *puny*   junior, minor
326 *indifferent gear*   the usual kind; dubious virginities, girls pretending
     to be virgins
328 *Her life is certified*   she has a character reference
329 *decay'd*   'fallen on hard times' (Parr)
331 *riot*   extravagance
338 *panders*   pimps
348 *weal public*   the state
351 *brands*   branding
356 *rapine*   plunder, violent robbery
     cozenage   fraud
361 *cutpurses*   pickpockets who slash purses
363 *dead palsy*   paralysis
364 *craves*   demands
378 *conformable*   consistent, agreeable
381.1 *above*   in the gallery
387 *light*   literally 'light in weight' but Joyless understands it to mean 'unchaste'

388 *quoit* throw ('quoits' are rings thrown over stakes or pins, therefore with possible sexual innuendo)

392 *chops* jaws
Is your brain dry have you dried, i.e. have you forgotten your lines

393 *Do you pump* have you worn yourself out

395 *sneap* snub

399 *Hoyday* from 'heyday'; expressing exasperation

402 *cockscomb* fool, idiot

408 *in* back on track, remembering his lines

414 *votes* prayers, wishes

426 *mother of her maids* chief bridesmaid, maid of honour

426–7 Diana, perhaps unconsciously, suggests that there may be no virgins at the Antipodean court.

433 *Apollo with the Muses* god of poetry with the inspirers of poetry

437 *Hymen* god of marriage

448 *advertisement* reliable information

460 *bar* prevent

465 *passage* channel

466 *'Slid* by god's eyelid, common oath

467–8 *serpentine generation / That stings oft-times to death* Luke, 3.7, and Mandeville, chap. 92, where he describes women with bodies like serpents

481 *domine* master – addressed to Quailpipe as a clergyman

487 *coat* profession

488 *shift* change
coat costume
for expedition to save time

489 *your own, due to your function* i.e. his cassock, surplice (in order to officiate at the remarriage of Martha and Peregrine)

494 *issue* result; offspring

497 *wrought* made

498 *competent* sufficient

499 *of late* recently

500–1 *drawn ... anatomy* reduced by medicine to a skeleton

502 *rear* restore

504 *Art* medical science

505 *proper centre* equilibrium
medium moderation

508 *authors* authorities
515 *carries* clinches
518 *recipe* prescription
536 *keep* occupy
540 *You're up* you're my prisoner
545 *watch* stay awake
546 *match* wife

5.1

3 *This* apparently a secret door behind the hangings
4 *narrow watching* careful spying
   privy posterns secret doors
5 *strangers'* visitors'
11–12 *betray me / From her* make her unfaithful to me
12 *out of* elsewhere than, other than
   travail worry, labour
13 *bare* mere
14 *But* rather than
   rankness stench
28 *fathom-deep* six foot deep
28–9 *to the scantling / Of* just enough to achieve. 'Scantling' in archery
   'applied to the distance from a mark, within which a shot was not
   regarded as a miss' *OED*, *sb.* 3b.
42–3 *see ... things* oversee everything that happened
61 *Brave* wonderful (ironic)
64 *In posse* potentially
68 *offer at* attempt
83 *o'th' order* of the order of cuckolds
85.1 *habit* stage costume
91 *had ... waggery* did you two not fool about
92 *facks* by my faith, honestly
98–9 *nor ... Nor* neither ... nor
104 *anon* shortly
106 *Naked* without an undergarment; clearly; freely; exposed; uninhibited;
   plainly; open to the naked eye, i.e. publicly
111 *mutes* (1) mimes; (2) faeces; Barbara takes the second sense
114 *That's a bull* paradox, self-contradictory proposition
114–15 *Thou ... play* referring to bulls' horns, the emblem of the cuckold

116 *That's a bull too* that's another absurdity (i.e. how could a mute roar)
117 *speakingly* eloquently
124–5 *things ... properties* literally stage costumes and props, but, with sexual innuendo, also genitals
125 *practice* rehearsal

5.2

The opening seduction scene is modelled on Volpone's attempt to seduce Celia in Jonson's *Volpone*, 3.7.189ff.

7 *Marcus* Mark Anthony
8 *she ... husband* as Cleopatra had before she met Mark Anthony
9 *friendship* love affair
9–12 *Had ... cause* Sextus Tarquinius raped Lucretia, chaste wife of the Roman general Collatinus. Her subsequent suicide led to a civil war in which the Tarquin kings were expelled from Rome. Cf. Shakespeare, *Rape of Lucrece*.
14 *Mammon* riches, or the devil who is their patron
Pluto properly Plutus, Greek god of riches
15–16 *let ... Danaë* Jupiter seduced Danaë in the form of a shower of gold
16 *outvie* outdo
27 *stamp* the effigy of the monarch (so that cutting it is treason)
clip cut or snip a part away
28–9 'Bribery in a capital case in law is wicked but to bribe a soul to damnation is worse.'
34 *demigods* children fathered by Jupiter with mortal women
50 *in full grant* to be all mine
53 *weigh'd* considered, valued
64 *pretending* claiming (not necessarily falsely)
zeal devotion
71 *This is not earnest* you can't mean this
75 *nip* pinch
76 *I'm past* I'm no longer
made no wanton not be treated as a child
81 *disposition* inclination, predisposition
92–3 *trifle time* waste time
93 *As* as if
95 *warrant* promise

96   *Which ... money*   on which you cannot raise a loan
       blank   bare
105   *yellows*   yellow was associated with jealousy
118   *try't out*   resolve it
126   *grudge*   scruple, unease of conscience
127   *here*   in her heart
       yonder   heaven
129   *relate you to your husband*   tell your husband about you
132   *dudgeon*   dagger with a wooden hilt
139   *stand*   vantage point
150, 336   *Shugh*   an exclamation of impatience (only example in *OED*)
154   *An oath of glass*   fragile, meaningless oath
163   *I ... child*   from the proverb 'it's a wise child that knows its own father'
176   *cross*   thwart
178   *on's*   of his
207   *change*   exchange, substitution
219   *match*   marriage
243   *have done*   sexual innuendo – have seduced Diana
260   *ready*   dressed
262   *no ho with them*   no stopping them
276   *possess*   inform
282   *settle-brain*   cure for a hangover
       drunkard's porridge   porridge was thought to cure a hangover
284   *toy*   trick
287   *anon*   at once
290   *flesh*   meat
       shambles   meat market (Turnbull Street was renowned for its brothels)
293   *in good sooth*   truly
296   *pregnant*   significant, meaningful
296–8   *so withal ... Plautus*   'and also so poetically correct, as I may justly
       say with Plautus'
       Plautus   Latin comic dramatist
301   *exact*   exacting
304.1   *lesson*   piece of music
321   *Fetch ... then*   in that case you cure him again
326.1, 336 SD   *untuneable*   discordant
328   *trains*   leads

331 *yellow jaundied*   yellow is the colour of jealousy – and jaundice the
      'yellow sickness' associated with the liver
332 *one horn*   associated with cuckoldry
335 *Conceive me this but*   understand that this is only
      device   artifice
344.2 *Mercury*   messenger of the gods
      Cupid   son of Venus, god of love
      Bacchus   god of wine and merriment
      Apollo   god of the sun and poetry
350 *matter*   substance
356 *spheres*   in Ptolemaic cosmology the most perfect harmony was
      supposed to be the unheard music produced by the movements of the
      heavenly spheres
      seat   throne
359 *revel it*   make merry
360 *this hemisphere*   the northern hemisphere
361 *disorders*   followers of Discord
363 *mansion*   house of Letoy
374 *pardon errors of my tongue*   reference to Barbara's assumption, at lines
      243–54, that Diana has been unfaithful to Joyless
376–7   behind this speech lies the proverb 'far-fetched is best for ladies'

Epilogue

380 *approbation*   applause, approval
383 *strokings*   healing
      seventh son   the seventh son in a family was supposed to be endowed
      with supernatural powers

The Author to the Reader

4   *pretended*   claimed
5–8   *Cockpit stage ... William Beeston ... Salisbury Court*   Though under
      contract to the Salisbury Court theatre, Brome appears to have written
      The Antipodes for another theatre, the Cockpit in Drury Lane, whose
      manager was his friend William Beeston, during a period of plague
      when he was not being paid by Salisbury Court.

Synopsis

The action of *The Antipodes*, apart from its opening scene, takes place in the London house of the eccentric Lord Letoy. He employs his doctor, Doctor Hughball, and his private company of actors, led by his chaplain, Quailpipe, to undertake the cure of Peregrine Joyless, a young man obsessed with reading about foreign travel to the extent of total neglect of his wife Martha, still a virgin after three years of marriage. Peregrine's father, Joyless, a country gentleman who has brought his family to London for therapy, has another source of unease besides his son's obsession – he is pathologically jealous of his young second wife, Diana. Unknown to Joyless, Letoy plans his cure too. Letoy's machinations are aided by the heraldic painter Blaze and his wife Barbara (formerly Letoy's mistress). Blaze's knowledge of his wife's adultery cured him of jealousy long ago!

Peregrine's cure takes the form of a satirical play, written and directed by Letoy, whose episodic action presents scenes from daily life in the upside-down world of the Antipodean city of 'anti-London'. In these scenes, the life and assumptions, social, moral and economic, of Caroline London are subjected to farcical reversals: old citizens beg gentlemen to father children on their young wives, lawyers refuse fees, servants control households, girls importune pretty young gentlemen for bought sex, senior citizens are sent back to school, and courtiers are coarse louts while tradesmen are natural gentlemen.

The play is watched by two on-stage audiences with quite different perceptions of it. The first audience consists of Peregrine and the Doctor. In act 2, Peregrine emerges from a drugged sleep to be told that he has travelled to the Antipodes. Gradually he is drawn into the action until, persuaded that he is King of the Antipodeans, he finally disrupts the play with his interventions in the name of English justice. Meanwhile, the second audience, Letoy, Joyless, Diana, Martha and Barbara, watch Letoy's actors perform their play about the Antipodes, in which the leading performer is Byplay, an actor with a poor memory for his lines but adept at improvisation, who attracts the interest of both Diana and Martha. Letoy flirts outrageously with Diana throughout, to her apparent satisfaction. A climax is reached in act 4, when the play is abandoned after Peregrine's interventions throw it off course. Peregrine is 'remarried' to Martha, now as Queen of the Antipodeans, and the couple are escorted to bed by the Doctor and Barbara, with royal ceremony.

Joyless, forced to spend the night at Letoy's house, wakes to find that Diana has vanished: she is with Letoy. The dénouement in the final scene both encompasses the cures of Peregrine and Joyless and adds some unexpected developments relating to Letoy himself and his relations with Diana before a masque, incorporating music and dances from the jettisoned play, banishes discord and brings all to a harmonious close.

TEXTUAL NOTES

This text of *The Antipodes* is based on the two copies of the 1640 quarto (Q) in the British Library (shelfmarks 644.d.32 and 162.c.13). Where it departs from them it has been checked against the reprints and editions of John Pearson (*Brome's Dramatic Works*, vol. 3, 1873), G.P. Baker (in C.M. Gayley, *Representative English Comedies*, vol. 3, 1914), A.S. Knowland (in *Six Caroline Plays*, 1962), A. Haaker (1967) and A.N. Parr (in *Three Renaissance Travel Plays*, 1995). Information about the press variants between other copies of the 1640 edition comes from the editions of Haaker and Parr: readings from corrected states of Q are described as Qc, those from uncorrected states as Qu. The following notes record all verbal emendations of the text, attributed to their sources, and a few other significant departures in speech prefixes (SPs) and stage directions (SDs) (but excluding minor changes in positioning of the latter). SDs of editorial origin are enclosed in square brackets but without attribution, as most are both necessary and obvious. Readings originating in this edition are designated *this edn*. Brome numbered his acts and scenes according to the neo-classical system that starts a new scene with every new entry. This fussy system (adopted by Ben Jonson for his Folio in 1616) has been replaced by the more familiar one in which a new scene begins only when the stage is cleared or there is a change of location.

Modernisation, as always, poses a few problems. In this play of travel it is not always easy to decide between modern 'travel' and 'travail' as the best equivalent of the 'trauaile' and 'trauel' of the original (which can be used indifferently for either sense). 'And' in the sense of 'if' is spelt as 'an'. The play is in blank verse, but often verse of a loose and informal kind. In prose passages and in verse lines where metre indicates that participial final *–ed* should be pronounced as a separate syllable it is printed as *–ed*; where it is not a separate syllable in verse it is elided to *–'d* (except after *i* or *u*, e.g. *cried, sued*). Two extended verse passages, near the ends of 1.2 (73–8, 88–90) and 5.2 (between 276 and 335), are mislined or printed as prose in Q: these have been relined as verse. In some twenty other places where the verse lining of the quarto is open to question it has been slightly adjusted in the interests of phrasing and emphasis. The ten speeches between 4.1.305 and 4.1.361 that are assigned in Q to a single

Projector have sometimes been distributed by editors among all three (or four).

SDs and SPs take the number of the line in which they appear, with an added number if the line contains more than one, e.g. 74 SD, 28 SP3. A decimal point is used in place of 'SD' for numbering lines in entry SDs, e.g. 98.1, 304.5. Entry SDs at the start of a scene are numbered by the act and scene numbers followed by 0.1, etc., e.g. 5.1.0.2.

Dedicatory Epistle

14   entertain it with] *Qc;* entertain with *Qu*

1.1

1   SP] *Baker; not in* Q
96.1 *Enter*] *Pearson; Ex.* Q
198   SD]   *Baker; Ex. 3.* Q
262   he] *Baker;* she Q

1.2

23   SP] *Pearson; not in* Q
75   that's] *this edn;* that is Q
      with all my heart] Q; withal *Parr*
85   SP1] *Baker; Re.* Q

1.3

1.3.0.2   *A . . . table*] *this edn; in right margin opposite lines 208–9* Q

2.1

1   SP] *Knowland; not in* Q
42   actors] *Baker;* Actor Q *(Parr claims that final* s *was lost by damage during printing)*

2.2

68   SD QUAILPIPE] *Prol.* Q
151   loves] *Qc;* likes *Qu*

3.1

24   there's a poet] *Qc;* there, a Poet *Qu*
135   SD *his head*] *this edn; it* Q

The Antipodes.

Act 1. Scene 1.

Blaze, Ioylesse.

TO me, and to the City, Sir, you are welcome,
And so are all about you : we have long
Suffer'd in want of such faire Company.
But now that Times calamity has given way
(Thankes to high Providence)to your kinder visits,
We are (like halfe pin'd wretches, that have lain
Long on the plankes of sorrow, strictly tyed
To a forc'd abstinence, from the sight of friends)
The sweetlier fild with joy.

Ioy. Alas, I bring
Sorrow too much with me to fill one house,
In the sad number of my family.

Bla. Be comforted good Sir, my house, which now
You may be pleas'd to call your owne, is large
Enough to hold you all ; and for your sorrowes,

B   You

Facsimile of *The Antipodes* (London, 1640), fol. B1.
Reproduced by permission of the British Library (162 c. 13)

139   More than at first] *Qc; not in Qu*
319   in it] *this edn;* in't *Q*
411   An't] *Knowland;* And *Q*
435   an't . . . an't] *Knowland;* and . . . and *Q*
444   Gentleman] *Baker;* Gentlemen *Q*
462   should, I say] *Knowland;* should say *Q*
480   SP *Prompter*] *this edn; not in Q*

4.1

20   SD MAID*'s*] *this edn;* her *Q*
131   SP3] *Baker; Wom. Q*
144   SP] *this edn;* 3 *Wom. Q*
145   SP2] *Parr;* 2 *Wom. Q*
146   Was] *Parr; Mansc.* Was *Q*
184   SP *1*] *this edn;* 2 *Q*
185   SP *2*] *this edn;* 1 *Q*
451   SD PEREGRINE] *this edn;* He *Q*
474   SD LETOY *remains*] *Manet Letoy. Q*
482   SP2] *Baker; Chap. Q*

5.1

49   prithee] *this edn;* pray thee *Q*
93   knowest] *this edn;* knowst *Q*

5.2

16   o'erwhelm'd] *this edn;* overwhelmed *Q*
48   ye] *this edn;* I *Q;* you *Baker*
109   deny it] *this edn;* deny't *Q*
115   prithee] *this edn;* pray thee *Q*
143   give] *Q;* gave *Baker*
185   in this house] *Baker;* this house *Q*
334   but, by] *Baker;* but but by *Q*
346   four] *Baker;* feare *Q*